God's renewal has been advancing in our nation, yet issues of race and equality have proven difficult to navigate. In *Renewal*, my dear friend Mike Hayes shows the biblical, factual and personal reasons why we must become reconcilers in this divided age.

Bishop Harry Jackson
Senior Pastor, Hope Christian Church, Washington, D.C. area
Co-Founder, The Reconciled Church movement

Mike Hayes and I have been friends for many years. In the pages of this book, he inspires faith-filled Christians to trust God and pray for the next Great Awakening. He makes it clear that Christians are here on a divine assignment as kingdom ambassadors, and the church must impact the culture in all areas. There is great hope for our nation—and each of us can make an impact by sharing God's love, truth and wisdom with conviction and compassion.

James Robison
Founder and President, LIFE Outreach International
Fort Worth, Texas

Our country is in desperate need of saving from self-destruction, but the children of God can change that course. In *Renewal*, Mike Hayes is challenging us to do just that — especially with the key of reconciliation which is essential to the survival of this nation.

Dr. Bernice A. King
Chief Executive Officer, The King Center
Atlanta, Georgia

God's model for the church is to change the world one life at a time. In *Renewal*, Mike Hayes lays out the path for building lives with influence that have the power and ability to shape culture. These practical steps pave a clear path for true transformation, even in the current atmosphere where everything is politicized, and racial divisions threaten to tear us apart.

Will Ford
Chair of the Marketplace Leadership Major, Christ for the Nations Institute
Author of *The Dream King* and *Created for Influence*

Matt Lockett
Director of Justice House of Prayer DC
Author of *The Dream King* and *Prayer that Impacts the World*

renewal

4 Ways to Change Your Life — and Our Nation

MIKE HAYES

MIKE HAYES MINISTRIES

Renewal: Four Ways to Change Your Life—and Our Nation
First Edition Trade Book, 2018
Copyright © 2018 by Mike Hayes

To order additional books:
www.amazon.com
www.mikehayes.org
www.cfnr.org

Published by Mike Hayes Ministries

ISBN: 978-0-9814550-3-7

E-book also available
www.amazon.com
www.mikehayes.org
www.cfnr.org

Printed in the United States

table of contents

introduction
Our Current Crisis

Imagine you are accelerating down the highway in your vehicle.

Five, ten, fifteen, thirty-five, seventy miles per hour and climbing. The momentum and adrenaline begin to snowball as your speed increases. Eighty-five, one hundred, one hundred fifteen—the scenery begins to blur and you feel the steering wheel vibrate in your hands. As you anticipate the upcoming curve in the road, you enter the turn . . . but slightly overcompensate in your approach. That's all it takes. In a second, it's all over. You lose control of the vehicle and a fatal crash ensues.

The potential for destruction—of life, limb, property, and other collateral damage—is dramatically multiplied by one primary factor: speed. An overcompensation of the steering wheel at five mph and at 155mph result in dramatically different outcomes. In many ways, this is a graphic picture of the world in which we live.

Right now, individually and collectively, we are racing down a road at an ever-increasing speed with carefree abandon. My concern, however, is that we as a society may be heading into a potentially fatal collision with an undesirable future.

Throughout the history of humanity, certain moments or times are inherently more important than others. We are currently living in such a moment—full of potential for breakthrough and blessing, or destruction and decline. We are a people in crisis.

Society as a whole is moving faster than ever and the phenomenon even has a name; it has been dubbed "the knowledge doubling curve"[1] by scholar Buckminster Fuller, who purports that the total amount of knowledge in the world is doubling in a matter of months. Just a year or two ago, knowledge was doubling at a rate of every three years. It's accelerating.

The potential for incredible things is now in our purview, but so also is the potential for disaster. From a spiritual perspective, the speed at which we live and are amassing information, coupled with the untethering of deep conviction and many of the values that established this nation, is a deadly combination.

Culture Shapers or Cultural Consumers?

Thousands of years ago, the Old Testament prophet Daniel recorded a prophecy that there would be a tremendous increase of knowledge in a future age (Daniel 12:4). Today, we are living in this very age! Unfortunately, our crisis is not the quantity of knowledge, but rather the lack of wisdom in knowing how to apply this knowledge to advance God's good in the world.

Knowledge is simply information understood; wisdom is knowing what to do with it. In our current cultural moment, it seems that knowledge *coupled with wisdom* is in short supply. God Himself declared through the prophet Hosea, "My people are destroyed for lack of knowledge." (Hosea 4:6). Simply put: what we don't know *will* hurt us!

This problem is not only unresolved, but even sometimes magnified in the Church. As a champion for the local church through more than 45 years of pastoral ministry, I'm deeply disturbed at her current condition. The culture is changing the Church more than the Church is changing the world around us. Instead of Christians being the called-out *culture shapers*, we've become assimilated *culture consumers*. We're just not moving the needle on cultural change.

If you were to go to many churches in America and interview the average member, you'd likely find many if not most lack basic biblical understanding about the nature of God and His requirements for righteousness. Not only that, many have no idea of core biblical stories that illustrate these eternal truths. But they've probably binged the latest Netflix shows or spent hours consuming talk radio. Entertainers have become our influencers, including in the Church. On matters of sexuality, marriage and gender, the culture has moved the Church more than the Church has moved the culture. Biblical absolutes and historical norms with 5,000 years of historicity are being redefined or discarded all together as relics of days gone by. And these are only a couple of examples.

Fatherlessness is another significant and tragic condition of our society that has greatly contributed to the situation in which we find ourselves today as a culture. Here's the reality: We are now at 60 percent of children being raised in homes absent of a father among certain minority ethnicities[2]—with the entire population not far behind. That's six out of 10 mothers raising their children without a man or a father's presence in the home.

The brutal consequences of this trend has indelibly changed our society—and we've barely scratched the surface with regard to the implications. We have never been at this level in our history. Growing up fatherless brings an entire set of challenges, disadvantages, and tremendous obstacles that children spend a lifetime overcoming—with dramatic impact on our communities.

A Vision Lost is Yet to Be Recovered

In spite of these disturbing trends, and others that we see daily in our news headlines, I believe the United States of America was God's idea, and that God has preserved America to this point for a special purpose. We have only to look back in history at the condition of the world before the United States of America was formed, chartered, and built. It was a much darker world.

America has been responsible for over 250 years of the absolute freedom in the propagation of the gospel. She has been instrumental in sending the gospel to the ends of the world. Even today, the U.S. sends four times as many missionaries annually as any other single nation.[3] And these overseas outreach efforts have done more than just save souls. In an extensive 2012 study,[4] sociologist Robert Woodberry showed the positive effect missionaries have had on nations:

> *"Areas where Protestant missionaries had a significant presence in the past are on average more economically developed today, with comparatively better health, lower infant mortality, lower corruption, greater literacy, higher educational attainment (especially for women), and more robust membership in nongovernmental associations."*

Don't get me wrong; I have a huge appreciation for God's unique kingdom calling on other nations as well. I've had the opportunity to travel and know believers all over the world. I have the honor of having ministry relationships with men and women of God in Africa, Europe, the Middle East, Asia—you name it. In that sense, I truly believe the kingdom of God is global, not just national. But I also believe America's calling is special and exceptional. Sin has always been present in this imperfect nation; we cannot fail to admit that. Yet America has also been an instrument in the hands of God to make the world a better place.

We read in Psalm 9:17 a word of warning: "The nation that forgets God will be cast down." Today, our religious freedoms are continually under attack in America. It feels like ancient history when public school students could start their school day with a public prayer. We still kill nearly a million babies in the womb every year, which is unconscionable and soaks our land in innocent blood that cries out to God.

Even in this wonderful place called America, there are wounds and scars that have the potential to destroy us if we don't change our ways. Second Chronicles 7:14 has the answer: "If my people who are called by my name humble themselves, and pray and seek my face and turn from their wicked ways, then I will hear from heaven and will forgive their sin and heal their land."

Did you catch that part about "humbling themselves, praying, and seeking God's face"? When we talk about interceding in prayer for the nation, it seems egotistical to some. The cynic would say, *You guys think you're going to make a difference? No one cares about your praying!* But we know that God does care, and He answers prayer. He says it right here (and in many other places) in His Word.

We know the mercy of God can be extended because God is, by nature, merciful. Scripture is full of examples of this, as well. For example, we can look to the story of the negotiations of Abraham and God[5] over the pending destruction of Sodom. God was going to destroy Sodom for its sin. Yet there were a few righteous living in that city, including Abraham's nephew Lot and his family.

Abram brought that up with God and negotiated it with Him, all the way down to ten souls. "God, if I could just find ten righteous, praying people in that massive city of Sodom, will you spare it?" he pleaded.

God said, *"I will spare it if you can just find ten."* I think that's one of the most moving, amazing stories of God's desired mercy and grace on a nation, on a city.

If you can find just a few praying people, I'll spare it. The importance of sparing America cannot be overstated, partly because of its historic role as a missionary-sending nation to the world. I believe it is in our future to continue to contribute to and lead this movement.

The Keys to Renewal

I'm sure you can see, not only from what I've mentioned here but also from what you observe in the world around you, we need renewal. Individually, as the children of God and followers of Jesus, we need to be renewed in our individual commitments and allegiance to Him. Corporately, our nation needs to be renewed in its focus, healed of its wounds, and redeployed in God's mission.

How can this happen? Our nation is renewed when her people are renewed. Really, you see, it's *us* that need renewal. If and when *we* are renewed in our focus, healed of our wounds, and redeployed in God's mission, then our nation is changed.

This book introduces a vision for personal and national renewal that I believe can be unlocked with four keys. These represent a vital four-part process that must be carefully prayed over, thought through, and acted upon. The order of the keys and the doors they unlock is very important because they go from one to the next. These four keys are successive and holistic.

1. First, we have to start with enough compassion and faith to become active in **intercession**. Through prayer, we stand in place of those in need, bringing them before the

throne of our Father. When we intercede, it brings us to see: *We've got things to fix.* It reaffirms our faith that the solutions are as much or more spiritual as they are practical.

2. We become agents of **reconciliation**, whether it be political rancor, ethnic strife, economic injustice, or in other spheres—we want to see these things reconciled, and we accept our responsibility to be part of the solution.

3. When you understand what you're praying about, that there are things to be fixed and God has the answers, it brings you to **education**. Believers should be the smartest and most engaged people in the room. God has placed us as His ambassadors in the world, to function as agents of reconciliation. We need His insight—along with His wisdom and strategy—to share truth with others in compelling, loving, and uncompromising ways.

4. Then, we become an **influence** for God's kingdom, whether it be collectively by the tens of thousands or one-on-one. When we start by hearing God's heart through intercession, operating as reconcilers, and ministers of the truth, our influence multiplies. We become a greater influence by taking this pattern and replicating it.

In the chapters that follow, we'll define each of these keys. Through victories—and sometimes mistakes—you'll see these truths come to life in pivotal moments and vital scriptures. We'll explore why each of us need to commit to this continuous process. And we'll see the doors that will be opened to us when we do. At such a time as this, God will be glorified as His sons and daughters follow this pattern for personal and national renewal.

the 1st key

intercession

setting our sights higher

Five years ago, we felt God telling us to change our direction at Covenant Church, the church my wife Kathy and I founded that is now pastored by our son, Stephen. Started as a small gathering four decades ago, today over 10,000 members in multiple campuses across the Dallas area call the Covenant family their home. Over the course of those decades in ministry, we have sent out many pastors who have planted more churches. Our organization grew and became Churches in Covenant, a network of churches nationwide united in Spirit-led relationship, accountability, and spiritual covering.

At the time we received this new direction from the Lord, our missions efforts were mainly south of the U.S. border. Millions of dollars had been sown into Mexico, Nicaragua, and other nations. We were mainly focused on Latin America and that region. After dialoguing with our leadership team about this change in focus we were sensing, and hearing their support, I addressed the church on a Sunday morning. "God is changing our direction," I told them.

I shared how we felt the Lord had told us to begin to pray for twelve gateway cities—notably, two were Jerusalem and Washington, D.C. And, as I related to our church family that morning, He was telling us to give the whole ministry in Mexico and Latin America away. We obeyed. We didn't keep one part of it and totally turned it over to the people who helped us build it. Then, along with our team and church family, we started praying for leaders and events in the gateway cities God had highlighted to us, particularly Washington, D.C. This calling guided our hearts. The vision began to grow.

At that point, as a pastor, I didn't have any idea that Kathy and I would end up in Washington ourselves. I really didn't see a lot further in some ways than just doing every Sunday at our church in Carrollton. We had just enough faith to set our sights higher than they were before, take the next step, and walk into that. Often these days we look back and say, "Wow, I didn't know it was leading to this." But God knew that all the time! As to how we ended up in Washington, D.C. today, I attribute a lot of the reason to faith, obedience, and a particular type of prayer called *intercession*.

Called to Intercede

The root word of the word *prayer* means "to ask." A time in prayer often turns to asking for forgiveness through confession, then to personal petition where we seek God for needs in our own life. We read the Scriptures in prayer, asking for understanding and revelation. And we don't need to feel badly about all that asking! Jesus Himself invited us to come to our heavenly Father and ask Him for the things we need:

> *"Ask, and it will be given to you; seek, and you will find; knock, and it will be opened to you. For everyone who asks receives, and the one who seeks finds, and to the one who knocks it will be opened. Or which one of you, if his son asks him for bread, will give him a stone? Or if he asks for a fish, will give him a serpent? If you then, who are evil, know how to give good gifts to your children, how much more will your Father who is in heaven give good things to those who ask him!" (Matthew 7:7-11)*

Specifically, intercession takes "asking" prayer one step further in that it is asking on behalf of someone else. To intercede in prayer is to actually step in for someone and stand in their place before God; I believe this is the deepest level of prayer there is. Intercession, of all the forms of prayer, is the one where *you* take responsibility. It's more than just saying to someone, "I know you're going through it. You'll be in my thoughts and prayers." It is, in a spiritual sense, stepping into the shoes of someone else that you're praying for. Sometimes this means going physically to the place where they are, as we were called to physically relocate to Washington. Lifting up vague or rote requests for help—like, "Lord, help Susie"—is not really intercession. Intercessory prayer is standing in for someone else, taking on their situation and feelings as my own.

In the New Testament, one of the great examples of intercession is the Apostle Paul. He became so committed to seeing his people, the Jews, saved that he made a shocking statement: "I am willing myself to go to hell if it would mean the salvation of my brethren." Specifically, he wrote to the Roman church, "For I could wish that I myself were accursed from Christ for my brethren, my countrymen according to the flesh" (Romans 9:3).

How many people or causes do you have like that in your life? It is a weighty calling to stand between a loved one and the place of judgment, pleading with God, *If it's going to be them, then it's going to be me too.* Would you do that for your family? For your spouse? For your church? For your country? This was the call to intercession we received for our nation, years ago, and the reason we are serving in Washington, D.C. today.

We are a national badly in need of intercession—for men and women of God to stand in the gap between the way things are and the way God wants them to be. But sadly, many in our nation today are materialistic and self-centered. When the fight starts, they're ready to run instead of taking up the battle.

Intercessors, on the other hand, stand fast and stand in. They put on the full armor of God and stand ready for the fight:

"Therefore take up the whole armor of God, that you may be able to withstand in the evil day, and having done all, to stand firm. Stand therefore, having fastened on the belt of truth, and having put on the breastplate of righteousness, and, as shoes for your feet, having put on the readiness given by the gospel of peace. In all circumstances take up the shield of faith, with which you can extinguish all the flaming darts of the evil one; and take the helmet of salvation, and the sword of the Spirit, which is the word of

God, **praying at all times in the Spirit, with all prayer
and supplication.** *To that end,* **keep alert with all per-
severance, making supplication for all the saints ...**
(Ephesians 6:13-18)

If we want to see things change in our nation—and in our individual lives and homes—with all our hearts, we must seek the will of
God—then refuse to waver when it is revealed. We must be willing
to stand firm for what we believe, to stand in jeopardy of our own
well-being if it means the well-being and saving of others.

Ultimately, intercession starts and ends with Jesus who took
our place, who made the ultimate sacrifice and paid the penalty
for our sins. Because of this, God "highly exalted" Him (Philippians 2:9), and we know from the New Testament that Jesus is
right now seated at the right hand of the Father (Ephesians 1:20).
What's He doing? The literal position Jesus assumes is "ever living to make intercession for us," we learn from Hebrews 7:25.

It means Jesus is standing in our place. Vicariously, in that
sense, we are seated with Him in heavenly places. When we're
not worthy to stand in the very throne room of God, Jesus does
that for us. Anywhere that Jesus is, we are. That's why, when we
intercede for people and situations and even nations, we are taking up and carrying out one of the primary functions of the ministry of Jesus, in whatever sphere of influence He has called us.

Entering the Capital of the Free World

In 2015, we were at a conference in Washington, D.C. with
Churches in Covenant. I was teaching that day and had a reve-

lation deep in my spirit: *In order to make any real change in the capital city, we are going to have to be willing to drive a stake in this region.* It's a biblical principle we see reflected in the journey of Israel. In Joshua 1:3, God made a promise to the nation about to enter the Promised Land. He told them, "Every place that the sole of your foot will tread upon I have given to you, just as I promised to Moses." I could see it clearly. There is a certain requirement of occupation in order to have dominion in an area spiritually. It's actual people dwelling in a real place.

We had prayed for the nation and its renewal. As a student of history, I began to realize the Northeast is the most historically important region in America. Within that region, Philadelphia has a rich history with Constitution Hall where our founding charter was debated and written. Important battles of the Revolutionary War were fought in and around Boston. And New York City was where the U.S. Congress first met. But one city remains the epicenter of government.

For two centuries, Washington, D.C. has been the historic place where America has become what America is today. All three branches of government—executive, legislative, and judicial—have their centers of power and decision-making here. Every U.S. President since John Adams has lived and worked at the White House. The Pentagon is the center of American military operations. The State Department coordinates with global humanitarian and religious freedom groups here. Thousands of federal employees work and do life in the capital region. It's where this great nation was built. It's where it all happens.

Before that point, I had no idea this vision would involve moving to Washington ourselves and becoming as involved as we are. The Dallas/Fort Worth area had been our home since 1976. But with His calling, God gave us a love for the city. I talked to the team about it and said: "We've got to find a place here to open an office." Forming a board of directors and refining the vision, it evolved into the ministry we serve today. The Center For National Renewal is an interdenominational, non-partisan organization that, according to our mission statement, "seeks to catalyze ideas and influencers through prayer, dialogue, and education."

We know there is no distance with God, and we can pray anywhere. Yet it's significant when we have a physical presence in a place. To envision what we're seeking God to accomplish, going on-site to pray, is an act of intercession. That is the calling and role God has given us in our nation's capital—and it is a ministry He calls all believers to in their own spheres of life and influence, to take territory for the kingdom of God.

Letting Go Enables Us to Receive

One principle of "taking territory" is clear in the journey of Israel. They had to dispossess certain mentalities and ideologies to possess a new land. For those who didn't—well, a whole lot of Israelites didn't enter the Promised Land.

For Kathy and me, we had to release pastoring our very large and much-loved church, which we'd spent years investing our hearts and lives in, and where we had many dear friends and ministry partners. This was not easy. But I've always recognized that nothing is forever except God. Our lives are in His hands. Everything changes, and everything has a season. That understanding helped us make the change. We had done a lot of preparation for this shift over the years.

You can only do so much planning; at some point, you have to jump. It's like when, for the first time, one of your children is about to jump off the side of a pool into your waiting arms. You can only do so much telling them what it's like. At some point, they have to make the leap.

We made plans and had raised up a great team. My son Stephen had worked with us for years, serving faithfully in many of the hands-on aspects of the ministry before moving into leadership roles. He started out cleaning bathrooms at the church and doing janitorial work, then moved into media and excelled there. He moved into youth. All the way up through the ranks, he knew the operation from the nursery up, all the while possessing the heart of a pastor and the gifts required to lead a flock. When the time came, it seemed natural. (When a God-given opportunity comes about, it does usually seem sudden—but we can have faith that it's really been in the plans for a long time!)

Besides needing to shift my view on our church leadership and my own role in it, I also had to dispossess myself of certain attitudes about politics and government. This is not a blight on any of the leaders who have mentored us in the faith. But some I knew had discouraged our engagement in politics, even in voting and civic involvement. They had no special interest in Washington, D.C., and I had never even been there in my early life. In fact, I was an adult and had been in ministry several years before I visited the nation's capital city.

Walking around in the U.S. Capitol, wide-eyed and full of a love for history, I saw it all there before me. A realization came to me about the reality of what happens in Congress and among policymakers every day. Before that point, it had seemed like Disneyland or Mars—a place you heard about but had never experienced. But when I went there and experienced it in a closer way, the overwhelming feeling was: *We can do this. We can actually make a difference.*

Again, I was encouraged by the precedents I found in Scripture for what I was experiencing. The Apostle Paul addressed this aspect, too, of his intercessory calling in his writings to the early church. He wrote, ". . . whatever gain I had, I counted as loss for the sake of Christ. Indeed, I count everything as loss because of the surpassing worth of knowing Christ Jesus my Lord . . . forgetting what lies behind and straining forward to what lies ahead, I press on toward the goal for the prize of the upward call of God in Christ Jesus" (Philippians 3:7-8, 13-14).

Like Paul, in order to receive what God had for us, we had to let go.

Intercession as Influence

Important decisions are made in the lives of people who are governing in the nation. It's part of why I believe God had us open the Center for National Renewal only two blocks from the U.S. Capitol: to counsel and pray with national leaders, and to intercede for them in real time, on-site, with insight.

During the week of the Inauguration in January 2017, on ribbon-cutting day as we dedicated the Center for National Renewal, a U.S. senator joined us to celebrate the opening. I found myself in conversation with him on the third floor of the new center.

At the time, what I learned was confidential though now it has been reported. The senator explained his situation to me and asked me to pray with him about whether to stay in his role as a senator or accept a Supreme Court nomination. What kind of move would that be for him? He felt like he leaned toward continuing to be a senator.

Here was a national leader making a decision that would impact his life and the nation. Being on-site with a physical presence there, I had access to him and to information that would help me pray with insight for him and our nation, in which he had a significant role. This is a weighty responsibility, and a wonderful opportunity, and one we don't take lightly.

I encouraged this senator to remember that a Supreme Court nomination is for life. As a senator, he could be unseated the next election — who knows the whims of the public? This prompted his thoughts. He told me felt he was too young a man to take a seat on the Supreme Court and then be there the rest of his life. He could be more proactive as a senator in bringing up issues instead of being seated on a court bench and waiting for issues to come to him. Our conversation meant something to him, and God used it to help give him direction.

In the Scriptures, every leader we read about had the influence of a man or woman of God. Pharaoh had Joseph to be a voice in his ear. A later Pharaoh had Moses. Barak had Deborah. Ahab had Jeremiah. The list goes on.

King Nebuchadnezzar, whom we read about in the Book of Daniel, was really like a modern-day Iranian or Iraqi leader (and by the way, he was based in that same part of the world). He was a bloodthirsty, despotic man. Yet during a captivity, where the Babylonians had taken captive the people of Israel, God raised up Daniel and put him in Nebuchadnezzar's life as a counsel. That relationship between the prophet and the king ended up being a critical part of seeing the Israelites freed.

A lot of the conversations we've had in Washington, D.C., and will have, involve providing kingdom counsel and godly representation. It's standing in for and in place of. And it requires a different mindset about government than we get from watching cable news!

When a Still, Small Voice Interrupts the TV Debate

One thing I've noticed, not only from cable news but also from the vast proliferation of commentary through social media, is that we have become a nation of critics. One reason for this is that social media in particular has allowed us to broadcast our opinions so widely. People often criticize one whose shoes they don't stand in. How this relates to intercession ties right into a lesson God has taught me recently: *it's impossible to negatively criticize someone you're genuinely praying for.* You just can't do it.

During the nomination process for the 2016 election, Kathy and I were watching one of the first debates one night. In fall

2015, there were still fifteen or so candidates involved. While Kathy was preparing dinner, I started to make my own mental list of likes and dislikes about each candidate.

Governor Jeb Bush, Senator Ted Cruz, Senator Marco Rubio, now-President Donald Trump, and several others were on stage. I didn't want to prejudice my thinking just because I knew Senator Cruz, who happens to be from Texas. But as he was talking, I felt the Holy Spirit speak to my heart, saying, *Support him.* Kathy and I discussed the word. God wasn't telling me Cruz was going to win, that he would be the next president or anything like that. The word was simply: *Support him.*

What I felt in my spirit even more was conviction by the Holy Spirit. I realized I was not assessing candidates the way I should, as a kingdom leader. I was sitting there trying to make up my mind about who I thought could win based on whether they'd be good or bad. This is no criticism of others, because I am not their judge. But I knew I had not seriously prayed for or about any of these candidates.

The conviction I felt came from the words of Scripture. Paul said, "First of all, then, I urge that supplications, prayers, intercessions and thanksgivings be made for all people, for kings and all who are in high positions..." (1 Timothy 2:1-2). He established that the *first priority* is praying for our leaders. Here I had neglected to pray for these men and women—one of whom would likely have the highest position in our nation.

Praying for our leaders doesn't mean we don't evaluate whether policies are biblically grounded. We certainly do, as we will discuss further on in this book. But as believers, I have to wonder if we're exercising our right to free speech either too much or with the wrong approach—and failing in our God-given responsibility to intercede for the leaders of our nation. To maliciously gossip, tell hurtful things, or respond with jealous accusations about national leaders is all foolishness. It is a work of the flesh. It's impossible to do that with someone you're genuinely standing in for in prayer.

Senator Cruz later dropped out of the race and didn't win the nomination. But that experience changed something in me. It was part of the preparatory work of God for sending us to D.C. I gained a new paradigm: instead of just throwing politics into the bin of *likes* and *dislikes*, the Scripture tells us to genuinely *pray* for leaders.

When we begin to pray for those that have rule over us—and who are running for office—it equips us in a different way to engage in government. I wonder how many of us truly intercede for our president, members of Congress, judges, mayors, police chiefs, and other leaders? If more of us were praying for those in authority instead of criticizing them, we would have a different nation.

That's why I believe intercession is the first key to renewing this nation—and our own lives. If we read carefully that "First of all..." passage in 1 Timothy to the end, we'll see something very important. It also has a promise! "[Pray] for kings and all who are in high positions, *that we may lead a peaceful and quiet life*, godly and dignified in every way," says verse two (emphasis added).

In other words, for citizens to live a quiet and peaceful life, there has to be some intercession for our leaders. So what does that look like practically? Let's find out.

prayer and the upside-down kingdom

Kathy and I always try to start the day with a thoughtful prayer, whether we are in D.C. or elsewhere. Routinely, we ask, *Lord, give me at least one divine appointment today.* It doesn't matter to me if it's a president, a family member, or an Uber driver. I just want to know that God led someone into my life and me into theirs today.

Scripture teaches us to "redeem the time, for the days are evil" (Ephesians 5:16). To redeem the time is to multiply it. If you spend time in prayer, it redeems the time. You feel like you have more of it. I know that doesn't make sense. It's like the principle of giving. If you give to others, then you have more. You're probably asking, *How is that possible? If you give it away, don't you have less?* But that's not the way the spiritual principle works. Jesus taught us,

"Give, and it will be given to you: good measure, pressed down, shaken together, and running over will be put into your bosom. For with the same measure that you use, it will be measured back to you" (Luke 6:38).

This happens by starting the day with your mind on the Lord. In the big picture, intercessory prayer is a tool that can provide more fullness of time, and particularly more opportunity to touch the lives of others, and multiply and advance the Kingdom of God.

Because people are busy, this is all the more important. People in our society are more lonely and disconnected than they've ever been. Even though we've got devices in our left and right hands, and we can touch the world with social media, we're becoming more lonely than ever. People need an intercessory friend.

If you want to give, invest some time in interceding for and lifting up someone else in prayer. Just see how God redeems the time for you. Your day feels longer. Your week feels like you've accomplished more. Time given is like seed sown. You'll have a harvest come back to you in the form of more time.

The way God's kingdom works is often opposite of our own ideas. It's upside-down. The Scriptures speak of us kneeling in prayer and even laying prostrate before God. From a position the world would call weakness, we enter a place of great power.

Intercession and Enemy Love

God intends for us to be difference makers through prayer. It means we pray for wisdom and blessing for *all* in authority. You may not agree with the President, Supreme Court Justices, or leaders in Congress on all the issues. Heaven knows, those facing great persecution in China, India, Russia, and the Middle East have a much more difficult time than we do in lifting up their oppressive leaders in prayer.

But just because we disagree with our leaders doesn't mean we don't demonstrate God's love to them and pray for them, regardless of their political beliefs and practices. For example, as a believer, I am really concerned about some of the moral issues we face as a nation, that politicians could make a difference on. One such central issue, for me, is saving lives being discarded through abortion. I believe we can never defend not protecting the unborn. I'm honestly not sure how any Christian can defend such practices. Some try to explain to me how they justify it, but that's still something I cannot comprehend. By the same token, I cannot comprehend being so religious that we feel we can't pray for, love, and minister to those who may be in a totally opposite place of understanding from us politically, even on a hot-button topic like abortion. In all circumstances, I am called to thank God, worship Him, and be His ambassador. I am called to the ministry of Jesus to stand in the gap between the way things are and the way things should be. It comes down to living out my calling through intercession.

In prayer, we stand in the gap for leaders as Jesus does for us. Jesus didn't need to come to this broken planet and get involved with broken people, like all of us are, in order to be God. He was God before He ever got involved with us. He designed a way of becoming one of us so He could intercede for us.

"There have been many babies to become a king, but only one king became a baby," sings worship leader David Phelps.[6]

That's what the King of Kings really did. Jesus started out as a newborn. He grew up in the flesh, suffered, bled and died, then was raised again. Ascended to the Father, He is interceding now for us. He is interceding for the whole world. He has love so big that He is as much interceding for the most lost person as He is for me.

Now this is a test of religiosity! If this sets off your religion meter at all, then you may have more religion than you do salvation. I have to be at peace with the fact that Jesus loves North Korean dictator Kim Jong-un as much as He does you and me—as crazy as his actions are, as treacherous a man as he is, Jesus is interceding for him! Before the Father in Heaven, Jesus is interceding for Kim Jong-un to come to a place of understanding and salvation. If we model our lives after Jesus, and everything about our lives is supposed to be like Him, then we have to challenge our own selfish mentalities.

We cannot have any enemies. There may be people who choose not to like me. But I don't have to choose not to like anyone. I can choose to love everyone and have no enemies. That's easier said than done. I cannot do it in the flesh. But by the Spirit, because we're born again, we can love unlovable people. We can intercede for those with whom we disagree.

"But if you love those who love you, what credit is that to you?" asked Jesus in Luke 6. "For even sinners love those who love them." Even the worst people can love those who love them. It really takes God's help to love those who don't love you back.

Jesus as our Intercessor loves us all equally and stands in for us, praying continually on our behalf. "Love your enemies, do good, and lend, hoping for nothing in return," he said in Luke 6:35. "And your reward will be great, and you will be sons of the Most High. For he is kind to the unthankful and evil."

There's no greater thrill for me than knowing that Jesus is calling my name before the Father. That's what it means to stand in for us. From the place of intercession, I've seen the power of God work wonders—not only in the nation, but in my own family.

"The Child Shall Not Perish"

One of the great manifestations of God's love and faithfulness is when He gives us a word in time of need when we're desperate. When things look bleak, all we can do is pray. And there is power in that. We've experienced this many times in our family, but I remember one time in particular when Kathy and I were expecting Stephen, and she was about three months along.

We had finished a day at church and had gone out that night. Kathy started to hemorrhage as though losing the baby. We put her in the car, drove home, and got her feet up. I called the doctor and described the situation. He said, "From all the signs of what has happened, there's really nothing that can be done by bringing her in tonight. If she's lost the baby, then it's already lost."

Both of us were speechless. Kathy lay down with her feet up, and some lady friends came to sit with her. In the midst of intense emotions, I went outside our house and walked in the side yard. On that clear night, I looked up and prayed. I asked God for mercy, with all the fears that a young dad would have. I didn't feel like God's man of faith and power; I was just praying desperately as a father for God's help.

God spoke to my heart so distinctly that I can hear it now like I heard it then. God said to me, *The child shall not perish*. I heard it so clearly, I stopped in my tracks. I went inside and told Kathy and those who were with her. I said, "Listen, I was praying outside. This is what I believe God said and we're going to stand on this. God said, *The child shall not perish*."

Now Kathy had some thought that maybe she lost a child. Who knows? Maybe Stephen would have been a twin. But we know that Stephen was in there; he hung in there and he stayed. He came to full maturity and was born. God's word was true. *The child shall not perish*. That word was so strong that it got him here in spite of those conditions.

Kathy and I reminded the Lord of that word when Stephen was 17 and was hit by a car while crossing the street. He had a head injury and was hanging between life and death. For twelve days, we prayed at his hospital bedside as Stephen lay in a coma.

"God, you gave us a word: *the child shall not perish*," we said. "It was good when he was in the womb, and it's good now when he's 17. He's still a child. He will not perish. You've got a purpose for him. You have a calling and destiny for him. We're going to fight for his life, and we know that You are."

Our family doctor and good friend, Tim Shepherd, came up to the hospital and visited while Stephen was in a coma. He looked around at all the machinery as the brain surgeons were deeply involved in a procedure. Dr. Shepherd is such a humble man of great knowledge. I asked him a question about something they were doing. He said, "I don't know, Mike—this is a pay grade above what I do. I don't know what they're doing. But we're going to pray."

It was touch and go. But God's word is faithful. God brought Stephen through and miraculously raised him up with no debilitation. And I believe to this day that a huge part of his healing was the intercession for his life made by us and many others who agreed with us through prayer, holding to the word of God that had been given. Prayer makes a difference—especially prayer in agreement.

Agreeing in Prayer

From many various traumatic moments in our lives when we've called out to God and have seen Him move, we know how God can hear one of us when we pray. When more than one of us prays, when we pray in unity and agreement, it's even more powerful! Scripture bears this out: "If two of you agree on earth concerning anything that they ask, it will be done for them by My Father in heaven," stated Jesus in Matthew 18:19. When there's agreement in the Body of Christ about a prayer focus, it's better. More is better.

At the Center for National Renewal, we recognized this and saw the opportunity for connectivity through multimedia, the internet, and social media. We decided to build a virtual prayer team that anyone, anywhere, in any nation could join. When they commit to pray, pastors and spiritual leaders also indicate people in their church or sphere of influence uniting with us. In this way, we've seen hundreds of thousands join us since October 2016. Over 400,000 people are currently praying with us for the nation.

One of the largest people groups we have praying for our nation is comprised of underground believers in Iran. That's right, almost 100,000 underground Christians in Iran are praying for the United States! Maybe it's because they know better than any of us what it means to lose your freedoms. They don't want to see that happen to us as it has happened to them. They are not free to worship openly in a Christian church. Yet we take that for granted here at home. People in that part of the world understand what privileges we have.

We believe this intercessory prayer movement is a work of God. In Acts 2, we see there were 120 people in an upper room, interceding and waiting on God. It specifically says they were in one accord, in one place. *And there came a sound suddenly from Heaven.* The Holy Spirit was poured out on them, with miraculous results of renewal in their community:

> *". . . that day about three thousand souls were added to them. And they continued steadfastly in the apostles' doctrine and fellowship, in the breaking of bread, and in prayers. Then fear came upon every soul, and many wonders and signs were done through the apostles. Now all who believed were together, and had all things in common, and sold their possessions and goods, and divided them among all, as anyone had need. So continuing daily with one accord in the temple, and breaking bread from house to house, they ate their food with gladness and simplicity of heart, praising God and having favor with all the people. And the Lord added to the church daily those who were being saved." (Acts 2:41-47)*

As we see in this descriptive account by eyewitnesses from the Book of Acts, the Church in unity and agreement was a powerful force. Luke's account in the Acts goes on to tell us that in this power of unity and agreement, the early church interceded, with amazing results:

> "'. . . grant to Your servants that with all boldness they may speak Your word, by stretching out Your hand to heal, and that signs and wonders may be done through the name of Your holy Servant Jesus.' And when they had prayed, the place where they were assembled together was shaken; and they were all filled with the Holy Spirit, and they spoke the word of God with boldness."

This principle is as true today as it was then!

On to More Keys

As powerful as the principle of intercession is, there are more ways the Church can access the power and presence of God. Let's take a look at more examples from Scripture, and at three more keys to experiencing renewal in our lives and nation. We'll see what happens when the Church takes seriously another aspect of the ministry of Jesus, *reconciliation*—another important key to unlocking the doors to transformation and renewal in our lives, communities, and nation.

Take Personal Action with the Key of Intercession

Take a moment to reflect on the key of intercession in your own life. For whom are you currently interceding? For whom do you believe God is calling you to intercede?

Is there a word from the Lord you have not seen fulfilled yet, either for yourself or someone else? For a situation, or for a community or our nation? When the Prophet Elijah received a word from the Lord that there would be a drought-ending rain, it didn't just happen. He had to bear down and contend in prayer until the word was fulfilled and the rain cloud appeared in the sky and brought the needed showers (1 Kings 18:41-45). The Apostle James reminds us of this principle: "The effective, fervent prayer of a righteous man avails much. Elijah was a man with a nature like ours, and he prayed earnestly that it would not rain; and it did not rain on the land for three years and six months. And he prayed again, and the heaven gave rain, and the earth produced its fruit." (James 5:16-17)

It is not enough to have good intentions; we have to actually do it. When we pray, we unlock the heavens and access the power of God for our lives, communities, and nation!

Pray with me:

"Heavenly Father, I thank You that You hear us, and invite us to partner with You through prayer in conducting Your kingdom business here on the earth. Forgive me for not taking up this responsibility as I should.

Lord, I commit myself today to lifting up the leaders You have placed in my life, community, and nation. I recognize they are flawed human beings like myself who are daily in need of Your mercy, grace, and wisdom. Please give them everything they need to govern well, and to fulfill Your calling on their lives in this season.

I stand in the gap between the way things are and the way You want them to be, Lord, and proclaim Your authori-

ty and sovereignty over every wicked scheme of the enemy against this nation, Your church, and my own life and family. I thank You that You are in control, and I invite You to move in our midst and transform us for Your glory.

I pray in the powerful name of Jesus, Amen."

the 2nd key

reconciliation

not hating is not enough

I am an unlikely spokesperson for the reconciliation message. During my early years, my parents and family members did not understand the unconditional love of God and struggled to extend grace and acceptance to others—especially those that were different from them.

Perhaps in some ways, I was like the Apostle Paul because of the culture I grew up in and generations of wrong thinking. I was one of the persecutors—until God convicted me and changed my paradigms. Specifically, He opened my eyes and broke my heart over racial prejudice in the United States, and in my own life. He gave me a newfound empathy for those impacted by injustice, and a new love and acceptance for people of other races.

This was significant. But it was not enough.

About a third of Americans today, roughly 100 million people, are considered practicing Christians, according to Barna.[7] Many of them say they are tired of talking about race relations. "Only a few radicals care about this," I've been told. "What more can we do? We've done enough." *I don't hate anybody*, they think sincerely.

But "not hating" is not enough. God calls us, as Christ's ambassadors, to be healers, to literally be agents of reconciliation. This is active duty! The Apostle Paul wrote to the Corinthians: "Now all things *are* of God, who has reconciled us to Himself through Jesus Christ, and *has given us the ministry of reconciliation*, that is, that God was in Christ reconciling the world to Himself, not imputing their trespasses to them, and has committed to us the word of reconciliation. Now then, *we are ambassadors for Christ* as though God were pleading through us: we implore *you* on Christ's behalf, be reconciled to God" (2 Corinthians 5:18-20, emphasis added).

If we are to take up this mandate seriously, we have to take real relational steps to heal the great rifts in our society—divides across racial, economic, and gender lines. Jesus illustrated this powerfully in His ministry. We must go beyond simply "not hating" to becoming proactive agents of healing and reconciliation.

A Comfort Zone of Convenient Sin

I was born just outside Columbus, Ohio. In the days of my parents and grandparents, the Rust Belt city of Obetz was driven by coal mining . . . and attitudes of prejudice just below the surface.

As I grew up, my Grandpa Luther—named after Martin Luther—was my hero. He was a professional baseball player in the 1920s. An engaging storyteller, he used to recount to his grandkids how he played with Ty Cobb and other stars of the era. I never knew if Grandpa was making some of them up, but they were always great stories.

Baseball was not integrated in any way in those days. There was a Negro American League that played among themselves, but whites and blacks didn't mix at all. Grandpa played prison teams, but he didn't play with people of color.

The prejudice that existed at that time is reflected in the film *42*, which recounts the story of Jackie Robinson courageously facing down racial segregation in the late 1940s. It was also reflected in the jokes my grandpa would tell, usually at the expense of people of another race.

As a child, I thought he was funny. I had no early conviction or recognition of racism. We just thought, *It's Grandpa and it's okay.* Only decades later would our family come full circle and recognize the injustice and diminishment that was being propagated by those jokes and attitudes. At the same time, God was beginning to write a story of redemption. It started with a family who knew nothing of the truth and hope found in Jesus.

My mother and father had not set foot in a church before they went to one to get married. They didn't find their way into one again until the early 1950s, when they were invited to a tent revival meeting sponsored by Apostolic Gospel Church just a few miles south of Columbus. My parents attended one night and were saved, and quickly became a part of the church's life and ministry.

When I was five, they accepted the call to Flagstaff, Arizona to minister among the Navajo Indians and help build a church.

Looking back on the timing, it's hard to believe how quickly all that happened in our lives. Other than my dad's short stint in the Navy, they'd never been outside of Ohio. Changing environments and callings ultimately forced them to deal with some hidden issues in their lives and hearts. I believe it is dangerous to live in a small circle and never be challenged by diverse people. God knew this and had a marvelous plan to pluck my parents from that small circle and unfold His bigger perspective and plans.

An Inkling of Injustice

I was raised in my formative years among the Navajo and Hopi tribes of Arizona. It's where my original and strong feelings came from about the evils of prejudice, as I saw first-hand the mistreatment of Native American people. When I was in grade school, the government bussed the Native American kids in to our school from the reservation. It was 60 miles one way, every day. Most of them didn't speak English and there didn't seem to be any concern about teaching them English. School administrators had them sit in the back of the class and doodle. They were not allowed to compete on any of our sports teams. After school, they were bussed back out to the reservation.

As a boy growing up, this was confusing to me. I saw the inequalities and mistreatment faced by these First Nations tribes. My conscience was pricked to the realities of racism that exist in this country. I can remember standing at the bus stop one day in winter. Flagstaff gets a lot of snow, and about a foot was on the ground. A

Native American kid named Tom stood next to me as we waited for our buses. A big and kind of overgrown boy, he was behind a couple of grades—as many were, due to the school policies in place.

Classmates teased him often, but this time was worse. Four white boys jumped on Tom for no reason, right there at the bus stop, and began beating him up in the snow. I couldn't simply stand by, so I jumped in to defend him—and ended up with a black eye and a bloody nose.

I came home from school with that shiner. Over dinner, I told my dad what had happened and why. I was only about 12 at the time, but I can still clearly remember that conversation. Sort of upset with me, Dad said, "Mike, I don't understand why you always have to get involved with the underdog."

I said to him, "You know what, Dad? I don't know either. But I have to do something."

Granted, I didn't know exactly what I was addressing or even what to do about it. But even then, I know God was using those feelings to formulate in me an understanding of how to address injustice.

As God's chosen instruments of reconciliation (2 Corinthians 5:18-20), we cannot allow the mistreatment of people who have been marginalized. The prophet Isaiah addressed this, and spoke of God's heart toward injustice, saying, "Learn to do good; seek justice, rebuke the oppressor; defend the fatherless, plead for the widow" (Isaiah 1:17).

We cannot stand by and do nothing.

Uniquely Created and Divinely Different

As Kathy and I have traveled and become friends with people of different ethnic backgrounds and cultures, our lives have become richer and fuller. The hearts of all people demonstrate the full spectrum of God's love and who He is.

The truth is that all the nations of the world have their origin in the heart of God. Race-based discrimination—or any discrimination, for that matter—grieves our Father, around whose throne we will all worship as one. In fact, in Revelation 7:9-10, the final book of the Bible, we catch a glimpse into this ultimate reality: "Behold, a great multitude which no one could number, of all nations, tribes, peoples, and tongues, standing before the throne and before the Lamb, clothed with white robes, with palm branches in their hands, and crying out with a loud voice, saying, 'Salvation belongs to our God who sits on the throne, and to the Lamb!'"

God loves the various skin tones, languages, facial features and other differences we see in the diversity of mankind! He created our differences because He enjoys the variety of us being different. Each of us reflects a unique manifestation of the divine image. Remember the coat of many colors that Jacob made for Joseph?[8] The many colors are what made it an extravagant gift. In those days, the average family involved in raising livestock only had robes the color of sheep's wool. Middle-class people could get their robes dipped in a single dye of some color. Rare and special garments were made from individually dyed threads, which were then woven into a multi-colored pattern. The value of a coat of this sort was its many colors. This is also true of humanity!

God had a purpose in establishing the people groups of the earth, referred to as "nations" in Scripture. We first see this in the book of Genesis, when the family of Noah came out of the ark. According to Genesis 10, the sons of Noah fathered seventy original people groups. To every one of them, God gave a distinct region, look, and other attributes.

Genesis actually tracks the sojourns of Ham, Shem, and Japheth, sons of Noah, as to where they settled. They were likely born with various ethnic differences. Ham means *opus* or "burned face." He was apparently dark when he was born, and many Bible scholars and Christian anthropologists believe his ancestors went on to form the African nations.

Shem is where we get the word *Semitic*. People of Jewish and Arab descent are believed to come from his lineage, and is why the term *anti-Semitic* speaks of prejudice against Jews. Japheth, the third son, is believed to have fathered the Caucasian people groups that came to occupy much of Europe and, later, North America. We can trace the sojourn of the original nations, but all of them came from God—uniquely created, divinely different.

Confronting Divisive Doctrines

Where God sees beauty in our racial and ethnic differences, the enemy draws distinction and makes division from it. This was the very thing I first encountered as a boy, living among the Navajo and Hopi tribes in northern Arizona.

By the early 1980s, I was becoming increasingly sensitized to this truth, and keenly aware of what was going on in society.

I began preaching on racial reconciliation in our church. As I studied for these sermons, I became more and more aware of how bad doctrines always lead to bad outcomes.

I found it astonishing to read accounts of how, in the younger days of our nation when slavery was practiced, white "Christian" slave owners and even their clergy tried to justify owning and torturing other humans. One teaching of those times, called "the curse of Cain" was prevalent in Southern churches in the 1800s, heinously concluding and teaching that black people did not have a soul. When they died, adherents believed they didn't go anywhere, neither heaven nor hell.

What dangerous deception when a doctrine is used to dehumanize anyone or any people group!

Some theologians and preachers believed in the so-called "curse of Ham." This was derived from a misinterpretation of Genesis 9, where Ham looked on his father Noah when he was drunk and did something mysterious. When Noah awoke, the myth purported that he cursed Ham to be black, and led to the conclusion that all black-skinned people were cursed. Some pastors who believed this doctrine had black congregants. They'd preach, "You're black, but you can be saved. The blood of Jesus can cover you." On and on they went, still believing people were black because of some generational curse. Yet that is a falsehood that must be struck down completely.

Other doctrines taught vehemently against what they called "mixed marriages," even making up scriptures saying it was against the law of God to marry across ethnic lines. Does this not seem ludicrous in view of how easy it is today to see the genetic make-up of our ancestors? Essentially all couples are comprised of people from vastly different backgrounds. Do a DNA test and you'll find incredible variety in your family line. From those original 70 people groups, there are now thousands of variations!

Seeing What's Invisible to the Majority

We had bad doctrines in the church then, and in some places they sadly still exist. Of course, most racists don't make an issue of how Kathy has Native American ancestors and I have German and Scottish heritage, and we married each other. Black and white is the issue they have.

One of the things I have to understand and admit is I've never been a black man in America. I don't know what that feels like. I do know that centuries of race-based chattel slavery and Jim Crow laws still have after effects in modern-day society. I don't know what it feels like to not have an opportunity presented to me, just because someone sees me as a person of color. Today, anyone willing to look at unbiased official data sources will find a host of arenas where black and minority families still face hardship in modern-day America.

Within the past decade or so, the National Bureau of Economic Research commissioned a study in the corporate world to investigate this issue.[9] It was an extensive investigative project, in which a team of researchers responded to job openings with two sets of résumés. "Applicants" had the exact same education and past experience, with only the names changed.

Census records were used to determine popular names among white and black families. They used Greg and Emily for one man and woman, as well as Lakisha and Jamal—names popularly given to black children. The research team applied to many hundreds of companies across the United States with job openings. They sent out over 5,000 résumés. Knowing no other information, companies gave 50 percent more callbacks to Greg and Emily. Those with "black" names clearly faced discrimination.

How many of our brothers and sisters of color are not getting a fair shake in the job market? It's little wonder why black unemployment has long been double the overall rate in most regions of our nation.[10] And that's not all. We haven't room here to touch on stats in criminal sentencing, education, housing segregation, and a host of other issues. The bottom line is: I don't know what it feels like to be *pre-judged* because of my skin color. That's where the word *prejudice* comes from. So I have to be sensitive, recognizing I've likely accrued benefits in life at someone else's expense. This is one step toward becoming an agent of reconciliation.

My dear friends and fellow pastors Gordon Banks—now pastoring near Seattle—and Ricky Texada of Covenant Church often enlighten me about these issues of systemic racism in society. These men are such family to me, such brothers, I don't even think of them as men of color. It's simply not my first thought. Yet when we're dealing with something strategically as a national network of churches, it's immensely important and gratifying to me to be able to turn to them and ask honest questions, like *"How do you feel about this? How does this sound to you? What does this look like to you?"* They can look through eyes that I have never seen through. It's really helpful. I don't think we do enough of that in the Church. In conversations, those of us in the white majority need to inquire about issues of race and ask what racism feels like, and what we can do about it.

The Three Prejudices in Society

The reality is that we have many blind spots, individually and corporately. This was the case even in the first century. One letter written by the Apostle Paul to churches in the Roman province of Galatia addressed three primary prejudices in their society. More than 2,000 years later, these sinful biases still exist in the heart of man, and in our society today.

In Galatians 3:28, Paul stated, "There is neither Jew nor Greek, there is neither bond nor free, there is neither male nor female: for you are all one in Christ Jesus." The first prejudice he addressed was when he said "neither Jew nor Greek." He spoke of racial or ethnic prejudice, often based on skin color, appearance, or a person's country of origin.

Second, he addressed economic prejudice. "Bond nor free" means some were slaves. We know the word of God in its totality does not uphold slavery, though that was a tragic reality at the time. In the modern context, some work for someone else while others have great wealth or work for themselves. It doesn't make a difference in the kingdom of God. In Paul's day, class warfare between rich and poor—with no middle class—was very obvious. God says there is no dividing line. His word is for everyone, whether rich or poor.

Third, the phrase "male or female" speaks to gender prejudice. We've come a long way in the last few decades on this front. Women now have the opportunity to fully develop their skills and abilities. Many have accomplished tremendous success in the corporate, academic, scientific, and other fields; some oversee broad-based, respected Christian ministries that bless millions of people with biblical teaching. That wouldn't have happened 50 years ago.

Now, the Church cannot take full credit for overturning gender prejudice. I'd say it started in the business and sports worlds, and then the Church began to recognize and uphold the value of women's voices—as Jesus illustrated in the Gospel accounts. Today, certain denominations and congregations remain opposed to women preaching, overseeing, or leading. There's still work to do in some circles, but by and large this has changed tremendously for the better.

Paul addressed racial, economic, and gender prejudice all at once. When we come into the kingdom, those biases of culture, past experience, and stereotypes need to fall away. But the first step often isn't even in our churches or ministries; it's in our own homes and families. And we start by examining our own hearts.

confronting racism

Without dishonoring my grandfather, I need to tell this story because it reveals several truths, and concerns how my extended family and I began to break free from the generational sin of racial prejudice.

As I mentioned earlier, Grandpa always told these yarns in which racial epithets were common—not publicly, but certainly in family settings. In his heart, I do not believe Grandpa hated black people. He just never connected how his hateful language felt to those on the receiving end. It's a strange phenomenon.

Gradually, as I grew in understanding of racial inequality and injustice, God's Holy Spirit convicted me about this double standard and I repented. But I had to take it a step further. I had to confront the reality of my own heart—then confront it in my family, starting with Grandpa. I went to visit him at a nursing home in Arizona. He had had a stroke and was not doing well.

At the nursing home, a young black man was serving as his orderly. The man came in to help with his bedpan. Grandpa looked at me and made a comment to this man's face. He said, "Mike, since I've had this stroke, I don't have my right arm—but I still have that left hook. I'm going to take this n***** out when he comes closer to me."

The black man tried to brush it off, saying, "Oh, Mr. Hayes, you don't mean that!"

My grandpa replied, "Yeah, I do mean it too." When he left the room, I decided it was time to challenge this appalling affront to this man's humanity. Grandpa had been my hero, so my heart was racing—but I had to confront him.

"Grandpa, I've got to tell you, I've laughed at your jokes in the past and looked up to you all my life," I began. "But what you just did was absolutely not acceptable and it's not good. I cannot abide allowing you to get by with that and say nothing."

He said, "Well, I've just always been that way, Mike."

But I wouldn't excuse it this time. I told him, "No, not always. Surely there was a time this bias started. Grandpa, you've been saved and have loved Jesus for over 50 years. Why hasn't that changed you?"

He said, "Son, you just don't understand things I went through."

I told him, "Well, I want to."

Grandpa went on to tell me a story I had never heard and I don't think anyone in the family even knew. It teaches me that no one is born hating people of other colors and races. We *learn* that behavior, and none of us knew where Grandpa had learned it. He told it something like this:

Mike, when I was about five years old, my dad was leaving the house one night to go join some friends. I cried after him and said, "I want to go."

He said, "No, you can't go."

You know we lived in Obetz, near Columbus. It was one of those small towns that had a sign as you walk down Main Street: 'No Coloreds Allowed After Sundown.'

As a five year-old, I didn't know where he was going. He went out the door and almost made it to the front yard fence. He opened the gate but stopped and turned around. He told his friends to wait a minute and came back.

"You know what, son?" he told me. "You're old enough to learn what life is about. You come on and go with me." He grabbed me by the hand, and we went down to the river. There was a large bridge that went over the river in Obetz.

A group of white men had three black men tied up. I watched as my father and his friends hung these three black men by the neck from that bridge.

That event, seeing three innocent men murdered, traumatized his five year-old brain. Something said to him inside, *I didn't know black men were bad? But it must be so because my dad and his friends just killed those men for being black.* He lived with this trauma growing up, and certain attitudes took root without any understanding why.

Grandpa wept after he told me this story. I cried and prayed with him. He repented that day, and committed to change his heart about this sinful racism, and I believe he did. He didn't live a lot longer after that.

The issue of racism in our family had emanated from my great-grandfather, and then through my grandpa. But that's where my generation broke the cycle—and a spirit of real reconciliation began to replace it.

I thought back to our ministry together with the First Nations people, when my parents left their comfort zone in Ohio. It was a difficult mission field where we all learned a lot. I saw such tremendous love in my dad—and also in Grandpa, who was Dad's first ministry associate. He did the baptizing of people and loved them.

God used Grandpa in fruitful kingdom ministry across ethnic lines, even with the baggage he held on to for most of his life. Those lies he believed had never been confronted. In those days, there was no counseling. People just buried their pain and propagated it.

It's never easy to challenge these attitudes in yourself, and then in your own circles—including your family. That was the hardest one for me. And I ask the same of you: do you see any in yourself, or in your family line? If you see these things, I encourage you to stop now, confess them, and repent. If there is someone God is calling you to confront, like I did with my Grandpa, pray for courage and timing and speak the truth in love.

Only from liberated individuals and families come churches that reflect true freedom in Christ!

God's Heart and King's Cause

When I was at The King Center in Atlanta, Georgia recently, I was reminded of how our society seems to forget that Dr. Martin Luther King, Jr. was first and foremost a pastor. "The church was very silent during my father's time and that was his number one issue," said King's daughter, Bernice King.[11] "What he called the 'moderate white Christians' were not getting involved in the struggle that he was in."

No one can deny how the Christian gospel was deeply embedded in the Civil Rights movement King led in the 1950s and 60s. All participants in the sit-ins and marches had to sign the Ten Commandments of Nonviolence written by Dr. King.[12] The first commitment reads: "Meditate daily on the life and teachings of Jesus."

One reason we have these persistent issues of race in America is because white churches, by and large, rejected Dr. King's message. Then as now, millions of Americans claim to be born again and read the Bible on some regular basis. Yet many Christians never recognized how our doctrines and power structures excluded people of color. We never mourned and repented. Many never changed.

So Dr. King went to Washington. Politicians embraced him; in some ways, they co-opted his message. They started changing laws, but you can't force love. The civil changes we saw were good as schools, workplaces, and the military were integrated. Still the church remained unfazed, with no spiritual solution spoken to society.

"We never really dealt with the issue of racism," concluded Bernice King. "We kind of swept it under the rug after my father's assassination."

King was violently murdered in 1968, fifty years ago as of this writing. I believe the Church's ongoing ignorance of these issues grieves the heart of God. If American Christians would act out the love we should have as disciples of Jesus and get involved in changing injustices we see, we would change this country. In thirty days, it could be a different nation.

The reality is, most of the 100 million of us are doing nothing. We go to church, sing, and preach to each other. Outside of our churches, we live in the world with our lips sealed. We say nothing, we do nothing, and we change nothing.

I believe this is one reason why our nation is not being renewed as God desires it to be.

Five Steps to Walking Faithfully

Race-related conflict has reached a crisis point in our communities. Today, 71 percent of black Americans and 52 percent of Hispanics say they have personally experienced discrimination.[13]

Following the tragic events in Charlottesville in August 2017, where multiple people lost their lives, many Christian ministers are beginning to wake up.

As Churches in Covenant, God has shown us the importance of preaching the full gospel to all and being a reflection of ethnic diversity in our local communities. Yet we still have a lot to learn—often from people who are very different from our own backgrounds. One uniting belief we hold in common is that Bible-believing local churches should be at the center of a civil, honest, ongoing conversation around issues of race, ethnicity, and unity.

In recent years, we believe God has revealed five steps to pursue biblical reconciliation. Rather than being "one and done," the opportunities to express each step often come in cycles. The prayerful intent in reconciliation is to respond to long-standing offenses, soften hearts, and create capacity for healing through real relationships.

The first step is **acknowledgement**, confessing how people have been dehumanized by the color of their skin. Jeremiah 6:14 (TLB) says, "You can't heal a wound by saying it's not there!" Racist attitudes—which are hurtful even if there was no "bad intention"—assault the very image of God reflected in each person.

When we realize the church has caused pain that must be heard, our next step is **listening**. "Let every person be quick to hear, slow to speak, slow to anger," states James 1:19. By hearing the personal injustices that have occurred and very real emotions, we can begin to empathize. This leads us to **repentance**, to "turn around." We choose loving actions rather than a passive stance. Only when we get to know our neighbors will we truly love them.

The next step is one I've seen led by my friend Bishop Harry Jackson and other Christian leaders of color.[14] In a spirit of **reconciliation**, they have called for walls of hostility to fall—even as we all recognize forgiveness as a process. To quote Dr. King: "The aftermath of the love method is reconciliation and creation of the beloved community."[15]

In decades of Christian pursuit of reconciliation, one last step has often been missed, leading to a breakdown of trust and lack of progress. This vital ongoing step is **restoration**, to challenge social systems of injustice and inequality. We choose to seek justice wherever our voices can influence those in authority. Our love cannot be silent or without action!

When Jesus saw someone hurting, He stopped for the one. Will we do the same?

Walking as Jesus Walked, Talking as Jesus Talked

We need to speak up and start reaching out with intentional actions to see things changed. The key thing for Christians is to hear God, fill your heart with the love of God, cultivate a passion for what you're sharing, and share it. Don't constantly second-guess yourself and hold committee meetings about everything.

I recall asking a trusted leader, a black man, what he thought when I addressed issues of race. He said, "Pastor Mike, that's not exactly how I would've said it. But I understand your heart.

I'll never hold that against you." He told me he recognized that sometimes he responded out of pain or reflecting his own bias. I also am committed to continue growing in listening and learning how to address these issues. The point is, we keep listening, we keep learning, and we keep improving. We cannot remain passive.

Society has paralyzed us with political correctness, locking us in to a place where we think we have to say everything right, often not knowing what is appropriate to say. So we say and do nothing. But if we choose to believe that everything that isn't said "just right" is because someone is a racist or has hate in his or her heart, then we'll never get anywhere!

For pastors, it's true that what we say can still be judged quickly and harshly. We need to guard against doing *mic drop* moments. Don't just drop a remark that could be inflammatory or misunderstood on race issues. Study the issues, know what you're talking about, know what the real challenges and problems are and tie it to the word of God. Then teach it that way. Speak carefully, knowing we will be judged by God for "every careless word that we say" (Matthew 12:36).

Deliver messages from a point of Scriptural knowledge, personal understanding, and current information—*always* covered in compassion. Be alert, educated, and regularly updated about racial, economic, and gender prejudice. Other biases surely exist. However, if we start with these three, I believe we'll begin an avalanche of healing and reconciliation.

But if we don't know the issues, and are not intentional about equipping ourselves and others to address them biblically, firmly, and lovingly, we will make little movement toward mastering the key of reconciliation. That's why we need the third key, education—which we will address in the next chapter.

Take Personal Action with the Key of Reconciliation

How did this chapter affect you? Did it stir any sense of conviction by the Holy Spirit about ways you, like me, may have vestiges of prejudice in your thinking and speaking? As I experienced, these roots can run deep and may have generations of history in your family.

Sometimes, like Daniel and Nehemiah did, we need to take responsibility for ourselves and for our generations (see Nehemiah 9 and Daniel 9), and ask the Lord for forgiveness and cleansing for our personal and generational sin. If that is the case for you, I encourage you to do that right now.

Then, we need to move in the opposite spirit of our past sin. Where we have operated in judgment and separation, we need to move in grace and inclusivity. Where we have participated in dishonoring conversation or jesting, we need to clean up our speech and use our words to build up and bless. Take a moment to ask the Holy Spirit to speak to you about specific ways He is telling you to change.

Pray with me:

"Heavenly Father, I ask Your forgiveness for all the ways I have not operated in Your unconditional love and mercy for all human beings. I also ask You to forgive my family,

including generations past, for ways we have violated Your truth and character, and for any way we have hurt or maligned any of Your children because of our prejudices.

Fill me with Your Spirit, God, and all the fruit of Your Spirit: love, joy, peace, patience, kindness, faithfulness, gentleness, and self control (Galatians 5:22-23). Let that fruit pour out of me into the world around me. Help me to be Your ambassador on the earth, to represent You will as an agent of reconciliation in every sphere You call me to.

I ask this in the name of Your Son, Jesus. Amen."

the 3rd key

education

educated and engaged

Over the past few years, I've spoken at dozens of churches and leadership conferences in every region of the United States. I've asked every audience a simple question: "Have you ever been to Washington, D.C.?" Without fail, by a show of hands, more than half of the people say no. Our government is supposed to be *of the people, by the people* and *for the people.* Yet most of us are content to just see the capital of our nation on TV rather than in person.

The imprint of leaders who believed in God's Word is obvious from the founding of the United States. You cannot go to Washington and not see it. Scriptures carved in the monuments seem to recall Jesus' words: "the stones will cry out" (Luke 19:40). The memorials, the Capitol Building, and even the Supreme Court testify of higher truths.

Seeing these declarations of truth gives us hope. Becoming educated about the history we possess gives us insight for current battles. What we're really looking for is the strength and weaponry to fight for another Great Awakening in America.

Revolution and Providence

The critical role of Christian faith in America's destiny stretches back to 1607, when the first settlers landed on Virginia Beach. They set up a cross on the shores of what they called the New World.[16] Thirteen years later, the Pilgrims landed at Plymouth Rock seeking religious freedom from the Church of England.

We see God's hand of intervention in the First Great Awakening, which swept through the colonies during the mid-1700s.[17] Before then, the thirteen colonies existed independently from each other. Some of them wanted to stay under the Crown's rule, while some wanted to fight for independence. There was not enough consensus among them to fight as a unit.

Providentially, the war for independence was preceded by decades of revival. Revivalist George Whitefield often spoke to crowds of over 20,000 people without amplification during the First Great Awakening. Hundreds of thousands of people along the Eastern seaboard were impacted spiritually. It brought the colonies together and focused them in purpose.

There are countless stories of divine intervention during the Revolutionary War era as General George Washington and his troops fought to be free from the oppression of the British Empire. In his book *1776*, historian David McCullough recounts one of the first great battles—only months after the Declaration of Independence was signed.[18] It came down to Washington and a few thousand men in a stand of trees.

The British had surrounded them and there was no way out. The Redcoats were going to kill them all. It looked like the end of Washington, and with him the dream of America's freedom. Then, mysteriously, a heavy blanket of fog came in from nowhere and shrouded the trees they were in. It made way for their escape. Washington later credited the providence of God with sending the fog. The strength of God was clearly upon early believers who sought religious freedom in this nation.

Today, history is being rewritten. It's an all-out campaign, from movies to textbooks to news shows. The other night, I saw a popular TV program that referenced Christopher Columbus discovering America. A comedian on the show said, *"1492, Columbus arrived here. Let the raping and plundering begin!"*

The new narrative is that Columbus and other Europeans came to America to rape the Indians, plunder their wealth, mine gold, and destroy the country. The education system teaches it to our children and young adults. The result is a Church that feels there is no exceptional plan or vision that God has for America.

Personally, I consider David Barton to be an underappreciated national treasure. He and his team at WallBuilders are a wellspring of historical knowledge about the founding of this nation—including the influence of faith and God's providence. If you've not had a chance to read his work, I encourage you to do so, as there is not room in this book to share its wealth of insight.

The bottom line: we have to see the whole picture and not shy away from hard truths. We have to know our history and understand its implications. We have to learn from the past to navigate the future.

The Shadows and the Coming Light

As American Christians, we need to face the dark seasons of our history as well as the great ones. From the early days of first-century Christianity, the beginning roots of racism came into the Church. It took the form of anti-Semitism in those days, as we'll address in the next chapter.

Then we move forward to the Crusades, and centuries later to slavery. Christians owned slaves, then perpetuated those practices by distorting and misapplying Scripture. The U.S. mistreated First Nations peoples, as we've recounted. These are ugly chapters in our history, and the Church continues to work its way through to a place of righteousness and biblical truth on these issues.

Yet there have been times of distinctly divine intervention throughout the chapters of this history. Thirty years before the Civil War, there came a Second Great Awakening. Revivalist preachers like Francis Asbury and prayer movements brought great conviction over the nation about slavery.[19] The truths revealed and espoused in these movements made soldiers and civilians willing enough to die so their brothers and sisters of color could be free. More than 600,000 Americans died in the Civil War, by far our nation's mostly costly war in terms of human lives.

As we believe for America's next Great Awakening, I want to strike a chord in your imagination. Could such an awakening address the breakdown of the family? Fatherlessness? Could it confront racism, bigotry, and hatred? Think of all that could be washed out of the fabric of our society by another Great Awakening.

Massive churches are being built right now in locations around the country. Yet it's rare to find a church that is moving the needle on cultural change. In fact, we may be digressing some in our moral stands as well as faith in the veracity and reality of the Word of God. We're building great churches but not changing the culture.

One of the earmarks of an awakening, as opposed to a local church revival or season of refreshing, is the cultural impact it has on society. The First and Second Great Awakenings brought about significant culture-wide change. The next Great Awakening is one that will shake America to its core, reverse devastating cultural trends, and strengthen the Church as a relevant force in society.

Citizens of Two Kingdoms

Many of us pray fervently about national issues and sins, and how badly we want America to change, and we should. Yet nearly as many do not see our place in society, or our civic responsibility, as having spiritual importance.

We are dual citizens—of the kingdom of God, and of the United States. We have responsibilities in God's kingdom: to pray, to love, to stand in for others, to give, to reconcile, to support. We also have responsibilities in our earthly nation, to lift up those that help us live in a peaceful, democratic society with police, the rule of law, fire and crisis response, highways, national parks, and other benefits.

In the kingdom of God, the highest prerogative is that we pray. In a Constitutional republic, the highest power we have is to vote. That's how a democracy works: the majority rules. John Bunyan authored *The Pilgrim's Progress*, a work that marked our nation's moral imagination for centuries. He once said, "You can do more than pray, after you have prayed—but you cannot do more than pray *until* you have prayed."

Now, I do not want to do any less than revere my spiritual fathers. But I was raised by leaders who didn't even vote. In some cases, they actually discouraged it. They said, "Voting is a carnal exercise that means nothing in light of kingdom realities and truth. We're trying to take people to Heaven; we're not interested in what's going on in the nation." Then I would read Scriptures that say, "When the righteous are in authority, the people rejoice..." (Proverbs 29:2). I couldn't reconcile myself to the contradiction. Isn't voting how we help place the righteous in authority? God's way in this democracy is to move through people who vote for a leader. We have the opportunity to elect our own leadership. So why not participate in that process?

Voting is where the process begins for believing that we can make a difference in our nation. It's the least we can do with all the benefits this democracy provides. Yet according to Barna, born-again Christians are today the least likely to pay attention to important public policy issues—even during election years![20]

If 100 million plus Americans profess to be Christians, why are we not living out what we believe in the public square? Kingdom responsibilities matter. So do our democratic obligations of voting, volunteering, being informed, and even running for office. It was Joseph de Maistre, an influential 19th century public figure who upheld the importance of faith in the public square, who wrote: "Every nation gets the government it deserves."

A Matter of Principles

Recently, this conviction was challenged as America was faced with two flawed candidates, forcing us all to look beyond the media circus and discern the principles at stake. Our nation was at a critical juncture during the 2016 election.

That election also marked four decades from the founding of Covenant Church in 1976. Because we've often discussed policy issues as a church family, we had strong rapport to be honest with one another. When the candidates were finally established, I heard people give a lot of surface-level criticisms. "I don't like the way she looks," or, "His mouth seems to sneer when he talks," they said. I thought, *Those are reasons for voting or not voting for someone?* In this critical moment, we had folks spouting nonsense. They were starting by looking at the *person* rather than the *principles*.

Some Christian friends of mine admitted they tend to vote more with their pocketbook than their moral compass. They were more concerned about: *Does this create jobs? Does this create government programs that give me more benefits? It looks like I'm going to get a raise on my job and free insurance, so this is my candidate.*

With all this in mind, and recognizing the critical juncture we were at, for the first time in 40 years, I did something I'd never done: I preached a two-part message on policy issues using the Scriptures and the two party platforms. I read through each platform, approximately 50 pages long, and noted the key issues. Then we walked through the biblical *principles*, what *policies* help society, how *politics* play into it, and then finally the *people* who were candidates.[21] I knew it wasn't my responsibility to tell people what to vote … but as a leader I felt it was distinctly my responsibility to educate them on how to do it wisely and deliberately.

All of us will, one day, have to stand before God and give an account of our values and decisions—you for yours, me for mine. One thing I can say for certain: as believers, we cannot sweep biblical principles under the rug. We have to uphold how God's Word defines marriage, take a stand for lives in the womb, and defend those who have been oppressed.

Frankly, I believe it doesn't matter as much where you stand on other things. I, personally, am an independent voter and avoid party politics. If you scratched out the party names at the top of the platforms, I would not care what party I ended up supporting if the tenets agreed with Scripture and with my spirit.

In 2016, the Republican platform was perhaps the strongest I have ever read.[22] Parts of it almost sounded like a Bible lesson. For instance, on marriage, the Republican platform had four pages on marriage as between one man and one woman. The Democratic platform in its 50 pages mentioned marriage one time, stating, "[All] Americans have the right to marry the person they love."

The candidates had sworn to support their respective platforms. So when you looked at the two platforms, it became not just a matter of who am I voting for, but *what* am I voting for here. This was difficult in a diverse congregation such as ours. In the current cultural climate in this country, it has almost become unacceptable to take any kind of stand for or against anything.

But we tried. We sought to understand each other, to avoid offense when disagreeing, and to keep walking in fellowship no matter what the election outcome. There was a higher calling at stake.

ambassadors in the public arena

You are called to be a kingdom ambassador. That role transcends any nation or political party, a God-given responsibility to represent the truth and authority of our Lord and King, in whatever sphere we are called to serve—whether a family, a community, a career, a church, or a nation. But it is not healthy to be so involved politically that you forget who you are, or whose ambassador you are.

No political party has a corner on righteousness and the left and right both have their good and bad. Liberals, for example, often have a heart to help everybody, including the oppressed and nations of the world. Conservatives often say in response, "We need to help people, but how are we going to pay for it?

The numbers don't work." This characteristic, adversarial relationship between the parties continually frustrates the process. I consistently meet good people on both sides of the argument.

Yet civil debate can also lead to compromise and solutions. God can show up in politics when unlikely allies choose to stand together for truth. That's why we should resist speaking in terms that sound like the Christian faith is somehow synonymous with any party. I suggest we shift how we think about politics. For one, let's vote! As we discussed in the last chapter, it's important to God that we exercise our civic responsibilities, and voting is the way our democracy chooses leaders. If there are, in fact, over 100 million Christian believers in America, the Church could be an authoritative voice for a higher way—but not with half of us never even taking 10 minutes on a Tuesday to go to a polling place!

Second, let's work toward inspiring, training, and equipping qualified men and women who are called to public office. Not only can we actually vote for leaders, but we can raise up leaders to vote for—godly people and statesmen rather than politicians.

Should fair, ethically sound policies on child welfare, marriage, criminal justice, prison reform, and all these issues really be up to career politicians who may or may not know or adhere to God's values? Or should these decisions be made by godly people who know what is right to do? That translates all the way up the line to those who could become our leaders at the highest levels. I am not personally called to run for office and will never run for any office to be voted on; my assignment is different. But I do know men and women of character and vision who are called to this sphere.

Strategies for reform can start from the heartland. Imagine a majority of men and women in Congress who care passionately about the future of this nation and generations to come, who are dedicated more to them than to party politics or self-interest. I've gotten to know some of these leaders currently serving on Capitol Hill and my prayer is that we increasingly see more of them.

To bring godly, qualified people to a place of responsible power will be a part of the next Great Awakening . . . one that will resound in the nations of the earth.

Compassion, Clarity, and Conscience

In the meantime, we often have to navigate a public arena of meanness and vitriol in which we strive to respect and love everyone as Jesus commanded us. He said, " You shall love the Lord your God with all your heart, with all your soul, and with all your mind. This is the first and great commandment. And the second is like it: You shall love your neighbor as yourself" (Matthew 22:37-39).

That doesn't mean your love shouldn't be firm, and it doesn't mean you won't disagree with someone about certain policies. How we do this makes all the difference in the world. Followers of Christ should reflect kindness and care—but we haven't always.

I am more keenly aware of this tension than ever, especially when confronting sensitive topics. For example, some years ago, I heard there were a few same-sex couples attending worship services at Covenant Church. I wasn't sure how to address it and simply prayed for God to give me wisdom and His perfect timing.

One Sunday, I made a statement during a message that was not a planned point, but which felt like the leading of the Holy Spirit. The statement was along these lines:

> *"Listen, I want to share something with you this morning. I learned that there may be one or more same-sex couples who attend and worship here at this church. I want to tell you how happy that makes me. We are honored that you feel loved and accepted by us, enough to worship with us and listen to the messages.*
>
> *I love you for that. I also want to tell you, that based on Scripture and God's will for our lives, I think there is a better plan for your life than what you've chosen. I'm going to love you and try my best to talk you out of the decision you've made, because I think there is better for you."*

It was said in love, which I genuinely felt toward these individuals. It was authentic. After the services, I did not have one negative response from those who attended, either who were in that lifestyle or other congregants. Perhaps it freed some people to express love to those who were different than them.

Because of what Jesus has done for us, our hearts are to be full of love for all—including people with different beliefs and views. But sometimes what happens is Christians get blamed for being bigoted because unbelievers think we're just sharing our own opinions, that we're somehow being "judgmental."

I beg to differ. I do not have the right to judge anyone, nor do I want that responsibility. I *do* have a responsibility to convey what the Word of God says. God's design for marriage, sexuality, and the sanctity of life are His ideas, not mine. If it just comes down to what we think, then we can do whatever is right in your own eyes. But I believe we're following a set of directives that are high above our ways.

America and the Apple of God's Eye

That being said, I urge caution about calling our nation somehow special because we are Americans. We have to learn to distinguish the bold, prophetic voice of God that speaks uncomfortable truths from nationalistic nostalgia.

Some people have a combination of our red, white and blue flag, the National Anthem, "Amazing Grace," and the Republican Party all mixed together as God's way and the gospel. Now, don't get me wrong; it's fine to be patriotic, appreciating our nation and military service members. But God isn't pleased with me because I'm a good American—or a good Republican or Democrat, for that matter. I cannot come to believe patriotism is one and the same as conversion. Only the blood of Jesus can save each one of us.

It's true that despite our failures and national sins, God's blessing has clearly been on the United States. This nation is a melting pot of the world, founded in freedom. And, it was destined to ultimately come to bless the roots of where we all came from. I believe one of the reasons God raised up America was to bless those referred to in Scripture as "the apple of His eye": the Jewish people.[23]

To be clear, this doesn't mean we support Israel politically in every decision. The Israeli government is a secular democracy and has made mistakes. Yet people often form their views from bad information. "Israel has been an aggressor against the Palestinians in the Middle East," people say to me. I wonder back, *How did you miss the fact that there are three hundred thousand Israeli Arabs who live in Jerusalem peacefully?*[24]

We have to start with Scripture. In Genesis 17:8, God told Abraham: "I will give to you and to your descendants after you, the land of your sojournings, all the land of Canaan, for an *everlasting* possession; and I will be their God." Part of the larger region known as Canaan, Israel is the only place on the planet ever mentioned in the Bible that God actually tied to a covenant.

With Israel, He made a covenant with the land to give it to His people and preserve it forever. I believe the special assignment of America is intricately involved with the survival and blessing of Israel. The heritage of Israel speaks to the roots of our faith—and the future of where world history will find its climax. It's one of the reasons that we bless Israel and God blesses us.

When Deception Breeds Devastation

A few years ago, Kathy and I were in Israel visiting an archeological site. An archeologist explaining the ruins before us was an expert known as the "Indiana Jones" of Israel. I commented to him, "You guys have archeology going on everywhere around this country. There are new things to look at every time I come!"

He replied kindly but firmly: "Pastor, you should realize we are not doing this so you can have new things to look at. With due respect, this is not for tourists. This is to prove our existence—that we were here before, and that we belong here. That's why we dig in the earth: to prove archaeologically that we have a right to exist in this land."

It was a powerful statement. As Americans, none of us have ever had to dig up archeological remains to prove we have a right to remain in our country—but that is what they face there. I believe it is an ongoing fulfillment of God's prophetic timeline.

Even though the Jewish people have gone through unbelievable difficulties for centuries, God has re-gathered them and re-established them in their land against all odds — that tiny country in the Middle East. God has miraculous power to preserve what He loves and what He promises He will care for.

God is a God of covenant. When God makes a covenant, He keeps it forever. God made a covenant with His people Israel. He called them out and chose them in order to show His faithfulness. It didn't mean that they were better than any other people. It didn't mean they were more righteous or more perfect; in fact, their mistakes are well-documented throughout Scripture.

Tragically, the Christian Church has perpetrated much evil against the Jewish people. In Acts 2, all of the early church leaders were Jewish. It began as a Jewish church that reached out to the Gentiles through the Apostle Paul. Yet from the first century,

Christian leaders started to attempt to separate us from the Jewish roots of our faith.[25]

By the third century, Constantine took over as emperor and leader of the Roman church. (He was supposedly converted, though I believe it was only a slick political move.) Constantine subsequently led the Christians in a mass persecution of the Jews.[26] The reason they gave was simple: *the Jews crucified Jesus, who is our Savior. Therefore, the Jews deserve to be killed.* They burned their synagogues and began murdering them. The central hub of Christianity moved from Jerusalem to Rome—without a single Jewish leader represented. Believers of Jewish heritage were totally kicked out of the church, leaving only Gentiles.

Many began to believe the false doctrine of replacement theology, also known as *supersessionism*. It essentially teaches that the Church, in God's heart, has replaced every promise God ever made to the Jews. Thus, it contends there are no remaining promises unique to the Jewish people, including those regarding the land of Israel.

In the 16th century, Martin Luther picked up and furthered this deception, and campaigned for Jews to be expelled from Germany. Historian William Shirer plainly states what resulted by the 20th century: "Martin Luther wanted Germany rid of the Jews. Luther's advice was literally followed four centuries later by Hitler."[27] Through the Nazis' horrific Final Solution, the Third Reich murdered two-thirds of all Jewish people in Europe.

Consider how one bad doctrine reaped destruction during World War II: the lives of six million Jewish people lost.

Holding Fast to Truth and Love

God hasn't replaced Israel with the Church; He loves Israel *and* the Church. But the doctrine of replacement theology is still prevalent today—in more places than you would believe.

As my wife and I were coming out of a theater recently, a man approached us, all worked up and red-faced. He said, "Pastor Mike, I respect you as a Bible teacher. But I am so disturbed by what you said about Israel recently. Why would you urge us to bless that nation? Half of them over there are atheists. Those who are Orthodox Jews don't even believe Jesus is the Messiah. Why would we want to support Israel?"

I replied, "Well, isn't that great?"

He said, "What?"

I replied, "Those facts you just cited."

He shot back, "No, those are awful."

I slowed down and pointed out calmly, "What is great is that God's promise to the land of Israel has nothing to do with the performance of the people who live there."

What I meant was that the covenants of God with the Jewish people reveal His faithfulness.[28] If God would break His promise to Israel because of their failings, then maybe God would break His promise to us when we fail. God has so freed us to love Him by our choice that even if we choose to say, *I don't even believe in you*, God still keeps His promises.

There are multiple reasons why we should honor Israel. God promised Abraham, way back in Genesis, "I will bless those who bless you, and I will curse him who curses you; and in you all the families of the earth shall be blessed" (12:3). He also commanded us to "pray for the peace of Jerusalem" (Psalm 122:6). Jerusalem is the place where Jesus ascended to Heaven, and it is where He will step foot on the earth again. I love the United States of America, but He is coming back to the Mount of Olives in Jerusalem—not to this nation.

Discerning the Signal over the Noise

God is leading us to have a different perspective than the world we live in. We must be careful about what news and information we watch, read, or hear. As for me, I don't take in a lot of foolishness, like spending an inordinate amount of time with talk shows that give the opinions of man. I try to filter everything through the Holy Spirit and God's Word.

A desire for that higher perspective is why we've started bringing groups of people to the nation's capital for a weeklong experience. When you walk the halls of power, you feel the tension and relentless pace. The spiritual impact that's needed in Washington becomes evident. When we take them on tours, people are wide-eyed seeing the city. The monuments and memorials etched with scriptures can be likened to the foundation stones of our nation. We have an intense four days where our visitors are exposed to important civics and history.

When they go to the U.S. Capitol, I see them impacted by the art and stories of what's depicted—from Christian baptisms, to prayers, to the bronze sculpture of Rev. Martin Luther King, Jr. Recognizing their part in the bigger picture, their hearts swell with pride as Americans and as Christians. We're even free to pray together in the Capitol, thank God.

We take people through the Museum of the Bible and the U.S. Holocaust Memorial Museum, both beautiful and moving experiences that connect the dots of historic events, our core values and current policies. These diverse leaders feel the enormity of it—and they generally encounter the presence of God at some point.

One place I see a lot of people profoundly touched is at the Washington Monument, the tallest point in the city. In 1885, its point was capped with aluminum—one of the most expensive metals in that era. It is inscribed in Latin: *Laus Deo*, translated "praise be to God."

It's moving when you realize this inscription was made many decades before the Wright brothers. Human-powered flight and drones were not yet invented. When all the scaffolding around the monument was removed, they intended that no one but God would ever again see those words etched in aluminum. It was put there for God's glory rather than man's eyes. I love sharing this remarkable national treasure.

Our tours end up at the Center for National Renewal where we share in prayer and fellowship together. Over dinner, these pastors and leaders tell what they felt and experienced over the week. They give testimony to what God did in them. Then we commission them as kingdom people to go forth and make a difference in their communities.

Without fail, their attitudes totally change. Some ask how they can bring people back to experience it themselves. Others will be called to run for public office. All of them become more responsible in their civic duties. These tours are a tangible way we are striking down certain mentalities that have prevailed in the Body of Christ. As dual citizens of God's kingdom and the United States, we will pray *and* vote, many tell us—and those are just the first steps.

The destiny of God has obviously been involved in our nation from the start. This nation was set apart as a place of freedom and worship for God's glory. We see the original intent… and now we're here. Sometimes we need to understand how far we've fallen.

How different could Washington, D.C. be if we imported the culture of God's kingdom into it? When people come who are filled with the Spirit of God, they leave a deposit in the nation's capital—even more so as new revelation comes to them.

We are called to this place as ambassadors of Christ: called to intercede, called to reconcile, and called to educate and engage. As we do this, the power centers of this city are being transformed, thoroughly immersed by our love for one another, our worship, and determination to do our part.

Take Personal Action with the Key of Education

How well do you know the issues being faced in your own community right now, and those being faced by our nation? Do you know what God's Word says about them? Do you know who is representing you in government and where they stand on crucial issues?

Find news sources you can trust, that will give the most unbiased view possible in their reporting, and combine them with reading commentary from a biblical perspective that will help you make informed decisions (and informed intercession!). To the best of your ability, I encourage you to be engaged in the civil arena as an informed voter and active citizen.

Pray with me:

"Heavenly Father, thank You that I live in a country where I can participate in governance of the nation through my vote and my voice. Give me discernment to navigate the virtual circus of opinions that exists in the public arena, and to hear the voices that are speaking Your mind and truth. Help me to reflect Your values and character in the ways I vote, speak, and influence others, and to be Your ambassador in this world.

Thank You for the ways You have used America in this world, and forgive us for the ways we have departed from Your calling on our life and nation. Give us, as a nation, a heart of repentance and a renewed vision and commitment to honor You and fulfill our destiny.

We ask this in the powerful name of Your son, Jesus. Amen."

the 4th key

influence

the mission our churches forgot

It was dark. I was following firemen shining their flashlights around—to show me the black, burnt-out remains of my church office.

The electricity had been shut off, and they had sprayed water on everything. The remains of books were still smoldering. The stench in the air was strong because of carpet, wood, paper and metal that had burned.

Some things survived. Fires always do strange things that way. I found my marriage manual, that little black book of cere- monies and vows I had received fresh out of seminary. I still have it today, singed on the edges. A few remnants from that fire help us remember what that felt like and looked like. What a violation.

After an arsonist attempted to burn down our church in 1981, God gave me a revelation for the first time. You can live and do church and teach and preach and sing and worship. You can do all that in a bubble. You're among friendly faces. Then you realize your message has gone outside the church's four walls. Everyone out there doesn't agree with you, like you or believe in what you're saying.

It was a reality check. *Am I willing to suffer for this message? Do I believe this enough? Is this just a Sunday sermon, or would I die for these truths?* I had that sense of reality. We knew it was worth it to boldly challenge certain bad doctrines—even though it apparently inspired this incident, as will be recounted fully in these pages.

The stand we took during that crisis paved the way for God to lead us to a place of greater influence.

When Faith Leads to Action

Washington, D.C. has to be one of the most interesting cities in the world. When I'm on Capitol Hill, the power of policymaking makes the hair on my arms stand up! Decisions made here affect the whole world.

Moving from Dallas to D.C. was and continues to be a leap of faith. I'm thankful for a healthy transition where Covenant Church is going on to great things, and we still have involvement. And though there are great challenges, Kathy and I are excited to be in this new season of ministry in our nation's capital.

We envision that the Center for National Renewal has a part to play in the narrative God is unfolding.

One reason for our excitement is the precedent we see in Scripture for this kind of ministry. A few years ago, we were touring in Ephesus (located in Greece), following in the steps of the Apostle Paul. We journeyed to Athens and Rome; then we made it to Corinth and Ephesus. We looked at the archeology of the churches he established—where the disciple John pastored and where Jesus' mother Mary lived out her final years. I realized on that trip that the places Paul went to during his ministry were the Paris, New York City, and Washington, D.C. of the ancient world. He went to the power centers of that era.

Today, the Church has mostly abandoned the great influence centers of the world to the powers that be. We've focused mostly on humanitarian missions while ignoring influence missions. Yet I believe we're half as effective doing one without the other.

Without disrespect to the importance of aid and relief efforts, I believe we will not move the needle on changing the culture by *only* working from a village at the end of a trail or feeding the homeless. Don't get me wrong; vital work has been and continues to be accomplished through Christian outreach. I'm not advocating that we abandon one to accomplish the other. I'm saying we must do both!

The modern-day Church's mission has often been primarily to places of great physical need. Humanitarian missions are wonderful and necessary. We should always be about giving food, water, and other provisions to those facing crisis. In fact, Churches in Covenant was well positioned to help serve the nation in 2017.

In my lifetime, we'd never seen such a year of national calamities.[29] Houston, the fourth largest U.S. city, was almost totally underwater. Florida was also majorly hit, followed by Puerto Rico; it seemed like there was a hurricane coming ashore every week! Then destructive wildfires began to rage in California.

I challenged pastors I knew across the nation to help alleviate these crises. Our own family jumped in personally. My son Stephen took my bass boat to Houston and starting rescuing people, alongside other pastors who did the same. They were right in the middle of it.

Through an effort called Help Churches, we all worked together to raise one million dollars in a matter of days. Churches in Covenant designated some pastors in the south Texas region to vet other pastors, find out their needs, and get them back on their feet. We did the same in Florida and Puerto Rico, then again in California when the wildfires broke out.

These kinds of humanitarian efforts are vital and will continue. But even as we help people who are poor or in crisis, influence missions carry the weight of God's purpose as well.

How do influence missions differ from humanitarian missions? While our vision continues to sharpen, my recent book *Influence: Becoming the Leader that Changes the World* dives into several secrets of leadership—including in this sphere.[30]

Change Minds, Change the World

We see many references to influence ministry in Scripture. One is in the Book of Acts, where in chapter 24 we read about the

Apostle Paul in Rome, the power center of the ancient world. We see him leaving his homeland—Caesarea in Israel—in shackles on a prison ship, headed for Rome to be tried and executed.

But he is not going to Rome for the reason he thinks. When he gets to Rome, they've lost the paperwork and have to set him free. Paul begins to minister the gospel and establishes a church. Just a couple years later, this man who landed in Rome shackled and shipwrecked writes to the Philippians.

A phrase from this letter is particularly telling. Paul ends his letter with these words: "All the saints greet you, but *especially those who are of Caesar's household*" (Philippians 4:22, emphasis added). How in the world do you go from being a prisoner, headed to a trial, to converting and pastoring Caesar's family? That's influence!

I'm so encouraged every time I see modern-day influence ministry in the Body of Christ. I remember one week after 9/11, a dark day in our nation's history, when our country was under a dark cloud of fear and trauma. Governor Rick Perry called together about 25 spiritual leaders from across Texas. I arrived at the Governor's Mansion with James Robison, founder of Life Outreach International and counselor to several presidents.

Initially, the discussion bogged down in crosstalk—until we realized what we really needed to do was pray! Robison came alongside Governor Perry and led that group to a place of interceding for him, our state, and our nation.

That day I saw the anointing of a father on Robison to bless leaders. We as the Church have this same kind of calling. But so often, we've left out those high places of influence that really need godly leadership. Or we're so busy with the detail work of ministry and humanitarian mission that we don't have time for influence mission.

The apostles recognized this tension in the early church. We can see their dilemma and identify with it:

Now in those days, when the number of the disciples was multiplying, there arose a complaint against the Hebrews by the Hellenists, because their widows were neglected in the daily distribution. Then the twelve summoned the multitude of the disciples and said, "It is not desirable that we should leave the word of God and serve tables. Therefore, brethren, seek out from among you seven men of good reputation, full of the Holy Spirit and wisdom, whom we may appoint over this business; but we will give ourselves continually to prayer and to the ministry of the word." (Acts 6:1-4)

Freed from the constraints of the detail work of daily (though important and necessary) humanitarian ministry, the apostles would be available to pray and minister the Word of God in the spheres of influence to which God was calling them. The rest of the New Testament narrative testifies to their success—and their growing influence around the known world.

For example, God told Ananias, whom He was calling to mentor the Apostle Paul (then Saul) immediately after Saul's dramatic conversion, that He was commissioning Saul to this kind of ministry. We see in the Scripture account: "But the Lord said to him, 'Go, for he is a chosen vessel of Mine to bear My name before Gentiles, kings, and the children of Israel'" (Acts 9:15).

For many years, I read that passage and missed an important detail about Paul's call to influence: Paul was called to *kings*.

"Gentile nations" and "children of Israel" speak of people groups. Paul was called to people groups and so are we. But right in the middle of that sentence — between Gentiles and Jews — God essentially says, *I am calling Paul to kings*. Rather than a national designation, this denotes a leadership role—a place of influence. God called Paul to kings because He wanted His kingdom represented at the highest levels of every government in the earth.

Influence missions are needed in the greatest power centers of the world: cities, industries, and institutions. But having kingdom influence at the gates of power does not mean a "dominion" theology, where we somehow mount up an army and take over. It's seeing everyone in my city as part of my calling.

Pastoring the Whole City

Sociologists have observed that people, regardless of their degree of civilization or sophistication, are tribal. It's become a common, good-natured saying that when we find a group of people with whom we feel comfortable and at home, we say, "I've found my tribe!" It basically means, "I've found a group of people I feel at home with." Certainly, the Body of Christ is tribal, for better or worse.

Churches have many different expressions; you might call them "tribes." Some are conservative, some wild and crazy. Some are young with tight jeans, some are not-so-young with clerical collars. There are churches with everything in between. Everyone should have somewhere to worship that is an expression they feel reflects an authentic offering for them.

We see *tribes* spoken of frequently in biblical passages about ancient Israel. The patriarch Jacob, grandson of Abraham, had twelve sons who became the nation of Israel. They were tribally distinct, with differences of appearance, culture, and tastes. Sometimes they had infighting among themselves, and disagreements, as brothers do. They came together for the cause of national unity and strategic defense when enemies came against them. They were twelve tribes but one nation.

The tribal nature of the Body of Christ doesn't bother me. We can have certain differences and still walk in unity centered on Christ and preaching the whole counsel of Scripture. What can be dangerous is when we become exclusive rather than inclusive—when we only know (or care) about what is going on in our little circle.

As a pastor, it's easy to have a tribal mentality. I remember thinking, years ago when leading Covenant Church, *I pastor this one church. I have a few hundred people and I know all their names, plus the occasional visitor—one of millions in our city. I'm responsible to pray for my little flock, teach them the Word, and love them.*

These people liked me, supported the church weekly and said my preaching was great. Sure, there was another pastor down the street who had more people in his church. Maybe that bothered my pride a bit. But I didn't have anything to do with him or them, because they had their church and I had mine.

Then God gave me a revelation. He raised my sights to the concept of pastoring a city, which is so unbelievably freeing. He pointed out to me that everyone in my city was within the scope of my pastoral anointing, calling, and responsibility. "But they don't all come to my church," I told Him in prayer.

And I sensed Him say to me, *They don't have to come to your church. Just change your paradigm. Act as though everyone in this whole city is in your church.*

Suddenly I looked at the other pastors in my city in a whole new way. They were my friends, not my competition! They were helping make my job easier by holding back darkness and bringing the light of Jesus to their part of the city, to the people in their spheres of influence. The people in their churches were allies, because my calling was to pastor the whole city.

This changed the way I looked at everyone in the city, even those who were not characteristically on my radar as part of my own "flock," even those on the fringes of our community, for whatever reason. After all, in any city, there are always some rascals. And there are people who don't know anything about the walk of faith or salvation through Jesus. But I can still be their pastor. They can draw a circle and leave me out—or I can draw a bigger circle and take them in. At whatever level they allow us, we can be a pastor to everyone. That's our calling.

This revelation brought me, and subsequently our whole church, to emphasize racial reconciliation in a greater way, looking outward to the whole harvest field rather than inward. We began to draw our circles bigger and bigger, and to encourage others to do the same. It was a time of significant personal and corporate renewal—and it did not go unnoticed.

Attacked for Preaching the Truth

I wrote earlier in this book about my own journey of understanding God's heart for racial unity and becoming a voice for racial healing—a journey I am still on. One story from the early years of our church, then called Faith World, was formative in helping me see why pastors must speak up for equality and unity.

Though our nation seemed calmer in the early 1980s than it had been a couple of decades earlier, there were racial issues in society we were not dealing with. In my sermons, reconciliation might be one point among several but never the focus of an entire message. Yet people were asking questions. Our leadership team realized we needed to address the undercurrents of prejudice head-on.

This led me to an extensive study of race issues in the Bible, and a six-part sermon series called "God's Purpose for the Nations." Many bad doctrines had been allowed to boil on the back burner of the Church in our region and others. I found it important to clearly address things like the "curse of Ham" and "curse of Cain," and strike down those damaging teachings and their collateral damage.

At the time, I was broadcasting five days a week on local radio, and used segments of Sunday sermons for those programs. The whole Dallas/Fort Worth Metroplex was potentially hearing those messages broadcast via radio. In the middle of the series, after I'd preached the third part, someone had obviously had enough.

Our church was doing early morning prayer with men at 6:00 am on Tuesdays. One morning when I arrived, there were fire trucks at the church. Some of the men had come early, about 4:00 am, and had smelled smoke and called the fire department. When they broke open the door of my office, the fire blew them back.

On my desk, I had a pair of eagles that were bookends for large concordances, made out of heavy bronze. The fire got so hot that one of them had melted like wax and run down on the floor. That's how intense the flames were.

By the time I arrived, they had the fire mostly out. Investigators recounted what they saw at the scene: "The arsonist gathered the notes on your desk and poured accelerant fuel on them to start the fire." Those included my notes for "God's Purpose for the Nations," so I had no doubt the fire was a direct attack against that message.

Then the fire chief told me something else, something remarkable. He said, "Pastor, the investigators think this fire started between 12:30 and 1:00 am, and we discovered it at 4:30. It burned for three hours but was contained just in this one area. The fact that it didn't burn the whole building down is a miracle."

I realized he was right. The fire had smoked up the entire building, but it had been contained within my office. That office was just sheet rock and a wooden door, but somehow the flames didn't escape. I had this immediate, overwhelming sense of God's covering and protective hand. All I knew to do was worship!

Right there in the parking lot, I lifted up a prayer of thanksgiving: *Lord, my fear and anger are overcome by the fact that Your hand was involved. When I was at home asleep and didn't even know a fire was being set in my office, You knew. And You kept it to one room.*

That event cemented two things in my spirit. It showed me there is real hate in the world. It also showed me God's covering. If you tell the truth and share it in love, the protective hand of God is enough.

I had nothing to fear moving forward.

Greater Influence from the Ashes

In those days, the city of Carrollton had something of a good ol' boy system in place. They came and did a bit of an investigation. There was never anything further done with it or anyone arrested—or even anyone questioned, as far as I know.

It really could have been anyone. We sensed it was someone who either sat in the services or one who had heard something on the radio they felt was inflammatory and acted on it. We did not hold a press conference. I made a decision at that time to keep it as low-key as we could. We trusted the deep work God was doing among us and didn't want to introduce a media circus aspect.

So, we made the repairs and the insurance paid the bill. The local paper did a story with several pictures. I finished teaching the series and we moved on. But something in the spirit realm had been triggered. More minority individuals and families than ever began to come to our church—black, Hispanic, Native American and others.

What struck me was that these folks were from people groups that had historically had a conflicted history in our nation. This confirmed a growing suspicion in my heart, that when oppressed people hear the gospel is being preached and they have a place they're welcome, they come running to that church! Our sermon series had also addressed so-called "mixed race" marriages. As interracial couples felt a place of protection, freedom, and respect, they began to come in greater numbers as well.

Jesus loves to minister to *all* people. Despite the prejudice of His day and even some of his own disciples, He would go, preach, and heal without discrimination. This point is often missed when we study the gospels—as I did back in seminary. In fact, I recall one day Oral Roberts invited me to his home for a Bible study. He had me open to Matthew chapter four. As we read, I got to verse 23, where it states: "And Jesus went about all Galilee, teaching in their synagogues, preaching the gospel of the kingdom, and healing all kinds of sickness and all kinds of disease among the people."

Roberts asked me, "What is the first thing there that it says Jesus did?"

I replied, "He taught them."

He said, "No, He did that later. What is the *first* thing?" I had to look at it a couple times. Even as kind as he was, Oral Roberts could be pretty intimidating. I couldn't get it and repeated my answer again.

"No, Mike—the first thing He did was *go throughout all of Galilee.*"

The great healing evangelist knew something of my heart regarding bringing people together. Roberts said, "That's going to be a strength of your ministry, because you are willing to go to all kinds of people." It continues to be my prayer that this would be true of Churches in Covenant and all expressions of the Body of Christ.

After the fire, our church grew exponentially—with people of all colors. Many apparently believed, *Ethnic diversity is right in the sight of the Lord. This is the way it ought to be! We cannot live under hatred and bondage.* People resonate with loving one another across the lines that often divide. This is an important part of renewal in our own lives and in our churches, and an essential aspect of our ability to influence our communities and nation with the gospel of Jesus Christ. As we resist being conformed to the thinking of this world and are renewed in our minds by the power of the gospel (Romans 12:2), we can change culture, and leave a lasting legacy of kingdom influence in our world.

passing the torch

Becoming a pastor to the city changed my whole life and how I looked at people in our region. I didn't want to treat people well just because they attended my church. I wanted to treat *all* people well, because they were within the circle of influence God had called me to.

Jesus taught us that "one who is faithful in a very little is also faithful in much..." (Luke 16:10). As we are faithful in our spheres of influence, God enlarges our circles. We may start out with a small prayer group, but, as we mature in faith and faithfulness, we may find our influence growing to a church, then a city, then the state, the nation, and even the nations of the world. The concentric circles keep enlarging as God enlarges our heart and our vision. It gets bigger and bigger. When we go where God calls us to, the impact reaches far beyond the local church.

Evangelist Billy Graham had worldwide impact. But he started from humble roots. In early 2018, the world lost a great Christian statesman and evangelist when he passed away. He lay in honor in the U.S. Capitol for a day, just down the street from my office at the Center for National Renewal.

I was struck by Vice President Mike Pence's tweet that morning. He recounted a story of being at a Billy Graham crusade in Indianapolis. His two young children responded to the altar call, and Pence walked down with them to pray at the front with a pastor. "That prayer made a lasting difference in their lives," he stated.[31]

The entire nation was moved by the memorial ceremony in the Capitol Rotunda where President Donald Trump spoke transparently about his own family's spiritual condition. His father, Fred Trump, had heard the message of the gospel at a Billy Graham crusade at Yankee Stadium. Though there would be ups and downs in their journey ahead, a seed of faith was planted in the Trump family that day.

I thought, *Billy was one young man from a family of farmers in North Carolina. God calls him to preach and raises him up. He reaches a point where now the President and Vice President of the United States say: "My family was saved because of his evangelism."*

This is the power of the gospel's influence—and of an instrument of renewal used in God's hands because of faithfulness to the call.

How Influence Addresses Corruption

As we hear God's call to understand the times and be involved in the public square, one question resurfaces: *Why do we so often end up with inept, corrupt, untruthful and downright immoral leadership at many levels of government?* This has sometimes been offered as a reason that Christians should stay out of politics and civil engagement. But I disagree. When I hear this argument, I point out an ancient story from the Bible:

> *"One day the trees went out to anoint a king for themselves. They said to the olive tree, 'Be our king.' But the olive tree answered, 'Should I give up my oil, by which both gods and humans are honored, to hold sway over the trees?'*
>
> *Next, the trees said to the fig tree, 'Come and be our king.' But the fig tree replied, 'Should I give up my fruit, so good and sweet, to hold sway over the trees?' Then the trees said to the vine, 'Come and be our king.' But the vine answered, 'Should I give up my wine, which cheers both gods and humans, to hold sway over the trees?'*
>
> *Finally all the trees said to the thorn bush, 'Come and be our king.' The thorn bush said to the trees, 'If you really want to anoint me king over you, come and take refuge in my shade; but if not, then let fire come out of the thorn bush and consume the cedars of Lebanon!'"* (Judges 9:8-15).

This haunting allegory details the condition that often exists today in America. As in the story, we inherently seek to be led. We see the trees in the story asking, "Be our king."

But when the olive tree, fig tree, and the grape vine all refuse because they aren't willing to leave their fruitful pursuits, the trees turn to the thorn tree. Only too happy to be asked, it offers only deception. "Come and enjoy my shade," it lies. Its sparse, prickly branches do not offer shade; its thorns only prick fingers and draw blood.

Then, revealing its inner lack of values and its ego-driven cruelty, the thorn tree says, "And if you won't, let fire come out from me and destroy the Cedars of Lebanon!" When the thorn tree doesn't get its way, its deepest desire is manifested. This worthless thorn tree threatens to destroy with its wrath the finest trees in the world.

This is a tragic picture of what often happens in leadership at every level in our nation. When fruitful, honest, faithful, values-driven men and women filled with character and wisdom refuse the offer and responsibility to serve, it opens the door of opportunity to the immoral, inept, and self-serving to step up. They are only too happy to fulfill their drive for power and recognition at the expense of the principles and values this nation was founded upon, which stand like the "mighty cedars of Lebanon." So we sit by as the cedars burn, set ablaze by "thorn tree leadership."

We talk about the days when men of character like Washington, Adams, and Jefferson sacrificed their *lives, fortunes, and sacred honor* to lead a fledgling nation toward greatness.[32] What about us? When will we be willing to answer the call to lead? How long will we chase personal comfort at the expense of national renewal? When did the "American Dream" become a life of personal wealth only realized by the super rich? What if we made our personal vision of the American Dream a nation filled with wisdom, kindness, generosity, justice, and mercy?

Can I ask you a personal question? *What about you?* Are your personal pursuits one and the same with your calling and divine purpose? The world cries out to be led. If good people refuse, those who only offer empty promises and pain are happy to take their place.

If you ever hear a call to lead, I pray you find the grace and strength to step up and say as the prophet in ancient times, "Here am I, send me!" (Isaiah 6:8)

The Hand-off

One key measure of our influence is the legacy we leave behind us. Though most of us will never reach the level of influence and legacy of a Billy Graham, we all play a role in the great generational transfer that's taking place right now between the Baby Boomer generation and the millennials. Every day, approximately 360 veterans of World War II are passing away.[33] Soon they'll all be gone.

Then the oldest of us will be from the Vietnam War era, which is my generation. I graduated from high school in 1968 as the war was raging. The Baby Boomer generation is now older and maturing. We have to be positioned to pass on our wisdom and authority—even as the next generation recreates our civil structures with new expressions relevant to the changing cultures around us.

This is actually one of the things I am most hopeful about: the up-and-coming generations. For me, having lived a few years, I can see some parallels between my generation and this millennial generation.

Post World War II, up until the end of the fifties, Americans were just living the good life with very little thought about the world or what was going on elsewhere. So many were blinded to the injustices in our own country. Then a confluence of events brought a generation to the streets to protest injustice: the draft, the Vietnam War, the assassinations of Dr. Martin Luther King, Jr. and President John F. Kennedy. I recall being a senior in high school, hearing that Dr. King had been shot.

The sixties became an activist generation of young people. Many revolted against what they saw as a bad war. The Civil Rights Movement enlightened us to care about fairness and a corrupt system. There was also Woodstock, where casual sex and illicit drugs flowed freely—with consequences that continue to plague our nation. With years of prosperity driven by secular undercurrents, we fell into narcissism and *me-centered* living.

Now, there's a generation rising up. This is a post-9/11 generation that cares about security, personal protection, and the protection of their family. They really care about injustice in the system and institutional problems that need to be addressed. Many have a conscience towards righteousness, justice, mercy, and compassion.

I am thankful for the rising influence of those in this generation. God has seemingly brought them into the Kingdom for this time and this moment. I see potential for another *greatest generation* to arise.

One of the greatest opportunities in the nation is to mentor and disciple the next generation. The last verse of the Old Testament, Malachi 4:6, speaks prophetically of this: "And he will turn the hearts of fathers to their children and the hearts of children to their fathers, lest I come and strike the land with a decree of utter destruction."

We have great potential with this generation. I'm encouraged by that. It's one of the reasons we went to D.C. and opened the Center for National Renewal. We need to become a force activated by the young generation—to help us prick the conscience of a sleeping church to the conditions that we can change.

The millennial generation and even Generation Z coming behind them are now being positioned to take over things one day. The hand-off taking place across generations is going to be done either with a plan or by necessity with force. What we need to do is get ahead of the curve by handing off the baton in a strategic way.

A young woman and friend in our church has run the 4x200 meters relay in two recent Summer Olympic Games. As I was thinking about this—the handing of a baton as a critical element in that race—I asked her to explain the process to me. "There is a ten-meter zone marked off with a start and stop line," she explained. "If you hand that baton off too early, you're disqualified. If you hand it off too late, you're disqualified. It has to be handed off within that ten-meter zone."

Running that part of the relay, she has to actually slow down, she told me. The runner waiting has to speed up. There's a moment when the two are exactly in sync—then she places the baton in the next runner's hand. I believe that Olympic athlete provided a picture of the generational transfer that's going on right now. So I pray, *Lord, don't let me do this too early or late.*

When I completed forty years of pastoral ministry in 2016, I realized it wasn't possible to do it too early. But I could stay too long at the same level and be too late. This is one reason I transitioned from the role of senior pastor and gave the leadership of the church to the younger generation, while Kathy and I moved on to our current assignment in Washington, D.C. What Stephen and his team are doing now, pastoring a local church and blessing the city, I did as faithfully as I could for forty years. I believe we've had a really successful hand-off of authority and anointing, as the next generation takes on its own approach to this calling.

Receiving Inheritance, Running with Influence

Now, by establishing the Center for National Renewal, our network of churches is driving a stake into the nation's capital. The great struggles playing out here in D.C. are worth engaging in, both spiritually and civically. We believe God wants His people in a place of influence at the highest levels.

Our new vantage point enables us to fly high over the battlefield. The intel we're getting, we are quick to pass on to the national renewal prayer network, as we all work together toward renewal in our nation and a mighty work of God in and through His Church.

I hope when you hear the word "church," you don't simply think of buildings or structures or denominations. Instead, when we hear "church," let's envision people from every tribe, tongue, and nation. Hearts ablaze with love, standing for righteousness and justice, believers are faithfully following God all over the world—including in the halls of power.

One former Congresswoman has become a good friend of ours. Now retired from years in public office, she is currently ministering in New York City while still often in Washington, D.C. When Kathy and I had lunch with her recently, she said, "Mike, when I'm in town, I cannot even go to all the prayer meetings happening throughout the Capitol building." Such fervency among Capitol Hill staff reflects the proliferation of what God is doing.

Recently, the White House hosted a small gathering of pastors and faith leaders. These leaders spoke with great concern of the events last year (as of this writing) in Charlottesville, Virginia, where three people lost their lives after thousands marched under the depraved banner of white supremacy. For this and other reasons, racial tensions continue to run high across our nation.[34]

A high-ranking official commented to me at this gathering, "Mike, Covenant Church has established churches with a hundred different ethnicities represented. They're all loving one another and worshiping together in community. Our nation needs that. How can we get what Covenant Church is to the whole nation?"

Those kinds of discussions are ongoing—which is one reason we are in D.C. The Church, when walking in its calling, has an inheritance of love and unity that our nation desperately needs in these difficult times. Our generation, because of the particular lessons we have learned and the life experience we have to pass on, is uniquely positioned to offer wisdom.

No one is saying the older generation is better. But because of the experience (and hopefully wisdom) God has added to our lives, we pray we can be entrusted at high levels with things God wants to address in our communities, nation, and world. What I'm doing in this assignment now, I could not have done as a 30-something. I am better equipped to do it now. You can't *learn* experience; you have to *live* it.

Emerging generations can start where we left off. I believe that millennials and Generation Z are going to be the greatest exemplars of the kingdom of God we've ever seen. They are better informed and zealous for justice. They have greater potential and possibility than maybe any generation ever seen. I can't wait to see what God does in and through them as they lay hold of the baton and run the next leg of this amazing race.

Take Personal Action with the Key of Influence

There is a two-fold scheme of the enemy against believers to inhibit them from fulfilling their call as kingdom influencers: one is insignificance, the other is pride. The first lies to us by telling us we are somehow *not worthy* of God using us in mighty ways. The second lies to us by overinflating our ego and telling us we are *entitled* to a place of recognition or influence. Either way, we have to get over ourselves, humble ourselves before God, submit to His calling, and trust Him to place us where He will for His glory and kingdom-building work.

You don't have to start big. In fact, you shouldn't start big! Start with the area right in front of you and serve faithfully. Perhaps it is your local church or school district. Your own neighborhood, office building, or family. Ask God to show you how He wants you to bring His love, truth, wisdom, and power to the spheres of influence He has placed you in. Then look for doors of opportunity to open for you to speak, share, or bring practical assistance. God will do the rest!

Pray with me:

"Lord, I confess I have not operated as a kingdom influencer in the way You have called me to operate as Your child and Your ambassador. I repent of my (insignificance/pride) and how it has prevented me from fulfilling my destiny. Father, please fill me with Your Holy Spirit; give me the courage and wisdom I need to speak and carry out Your truth and ministry.

I bless the generations that have gone before me, and the ones that are coming after me. I commit myself to faithfully carrying the baton for my leg of the race, and passing it off successfully to the next generation. I pray for them, Lord, and ask You to preserve and protect them in the increasingly difficult times that are facing the world they are entering. Give them increased knowledge of You and Your ways; bring about the Great Awakening in this nation that will empower them and inspire them to follow You, change the world, and usher in that great day when You return and fully establish Your kingdom here on the earth.

I pray in the powerful name of Your Son and my Savior, Jesus. Amen."

afterword

There's A New World Coming!

There is no doubt that, in the war to change the world, we will lose some battles—but we will win the war! As we close out this book, I want to be sure that you receive the most uplifting, encouraging word that you ever imagined. Make no mistake, the battle to see the world restored has been raging ever since the fall of man in the Garden of Eden. God had a glorious plan for the human race to live in peace and harmony and enjoy the best that life had to give. When Eve, then Adam, made the choice to disobey God's simple command to not allow them to eat from the "tree of knowledge of good and evil," we lost it all. The garden, the communion with God, the promise of eternal life—all of it.

So, the narrative then becomes a story of restoration, of renewal. In its first three chapters, the Bible tells how man has already fallen from God's favor, and in its last three chapters, in the Book of Revelation, God finally accomplishes the restoration of all things. The entire rest of the Bible is the difficult, treacherous, deadly but victorious story of God working a plan to redeem what was lost. This single truth should fill you, and all of us, with hope. God is going to fix everything that is broken! And it's going to happen relatively soon, in virtually a matter of moments! Let me share with you two beautiful Scripture passages that illustrate what I'm saying.

Soon after the birth of the Church in the Book of Acts, Peter was preaching to a crowd of people explaining the recent events they had witnessed. He explained that Jesus, the Messiah, who had recently been crucified and resurrected, had ascended up to heaven.

He went on to tell the rest of them (and ultimately us) who remained here on earth that part of their role was to "repent," which means to change your mind and go in the opposite direction, so that God would send "times of refreshing" (Acts 3:19-20). The word "times" used is the Greek word *kairos*, which is interpreted "divine interruptions in chronological time." In other words, *God will respond to a repentant heart and interrupt the natural order of events in time and release blessing in the middle of our struggles.* That is good news! The challenge with this, however, is that it is a "season of refreshing," but the war continues.

Seasons of Refreshing

When I was in college in the sixties, a number of my friends joined the army or were drafted into service and went to fight in the Vietnam War. Every six months they would be sent to Hawaii from the battlefield for what the military called R&R, "Rest and Recuperation." If they were married, their spouse would join them for a few days of bliss in the tropical paradise. It was a welcome reprieve from the horrors of battle. The only problem was, the war was not over! After a couple weeks of sun, sand, and their sweetheart, it was back on the troop transport and into the battle. The greatest desire of a warrior was not R&R in Hawaii but a victorious end to the war.

The same goes for every believer who is battling against spiritual darkness and working for renewal and reconciliation. When we become battle weary, we repent, renew our minds, and enjoy a season of refreshing. It is wonderful when those seasons come, and we always hate seeing them leave. But our greatest longing is for the war to be won. That day is coming but will not happen until Messiah returns. The Apostle Peter promised:

> *Repent, then, and turn to God, so that your sins may be wiped out, that times of refreshing may come from the Lord, and that he may send the Messiah, who has been appointed for you—even Jesus. Heaven must receive <u>him until the time comes for God to restore everything</u>, as he promised long ago through his holy prophets. (Acts 3:19-21, emphasis added)*

When Jesus does return, He will restore all things. The Greek word for "restore" used here in Acts is *apakotastasis,* which means the total and immediate restoration of everything that was broken, at the beginning. Finally, total and complete renewal!

When Jesus returns to Jerusalem and sets foot on the Mount of Olives, Scripture tells us, He will govern the "new earth," as the

Apostle John describes in Revelation 21. This is what the Bible calls the *parousia,* the glorious second appearing of Jesus. The first time He came as the baby in a manger, the Lamb of God. The second time He returns as victorious conqueror, the Lion of Judah. This is our blessed hope.

There is a day coming when we win the war. Until then we battle—not "flesh and blood," but "principalities, powers and rulers of darkness" (Ephesians 6:12). This is not a fight between Democrat or Republican, rich or poor, or among ethnic groups. This is a battle between right and wrong, light and darkness, belief and unbelief.

So, I encourage you—until that glorious day of total renewal—FIGHT ON! We may lose some battles, but we will win the war. Sometimes weary, sometimes lonely, sometimes wounded, but always believing, we anticipate that glorious day. It may be our generation or the next, but we never quit working, restoring, believing, and behaving like we know that eventually we will win. Never forget the awesome privilege it is to be a small part of the greatest cause that we could ever be involved in helping accomplish!

Finishing Strong

In the introduction of this book, I shared an analogy about a rapidly-accelerating car approaching a dangerous curve in the road, and how this relates to the pace of disastrous change in our culture. I do believe we live in strategic times, and that the Church is uniquely positioned to help avert a tragic crash in our society.

But we are not driving aimlessly on the road to nowhere. We are, in fact, in a race, and there is a finish line. Scripture tells us to ". . . run *with endurance* the race that is set before us, looking unto Jesus, the author and finisher of *our* faith . . ." (Hebrews 12:1-2). We must pick up the torch, or the baton, and faithfully complete our leg of the race.

To pull another analogy from Scripture, we also stand in front of a door. The Lord told the faithful church of Philadelphia, in Revelation 3:8, " "See, I have set before you an open door, and no one can shut it; for you have a little strength, have kept My word, and have not denied My name." How do we access that open door? The keys are in His Word.

I've tried in this book to highlight some of the keys I believe are the ones that help unlock the door to transformation and renewal in our lives and nation. I hope and pray you learn to use them. As you do, I pray you will experience the power and presence of God in your life, your family, your church, and community—and in this marvelous nation we are blessed to call home.

endnotes

1. Rosenberg, Marc, "The Coming Knowledge Tsunami," Learning Solutions Magazine, October 2017, https://www.learningsolutionsmag.com/articles/2468/marc-my-words-the-coming-knowledge-tsunami

2. "Children in Single-Parent Families by Race," Kids Count, updated January 2017, https://tinyurl.com/ChildrenSingle-ParentHomes

3. Jaffarian, Michael, Global Mission Handbook: A Guide for Crosscultural Service, InterVarsity Press, 2009.

4. Woodberry, Robert, "The Missionary Roots of Liberal Democracy," American Political Science Review, May 2012,

http://www.academia.edu/2128659/The_Missionary_
Roots_of_Liberal_Democracy

5   See Genesis 18-19

6   Phelps, David, "One King," Word Records, 2007.

7   "The State of the Church 2016," The Barna Group, Sept. 15, 2016, https://www.barna.com/research/state-church-2016/

8   See Genesis 37

9   "Are Emily and Greg More Employable than Lakisha and Jamal?", National Bureau of Economic Research, July 2003, http://www.nber.org/papers/w9873

10   "Unemployment of black and Hispanic workers remains high relative to white workers," Economic Policy Institute, Jan. 3, 2018, https://www.epi.org/publication/unemployment-of-black-and-hispanic-workers-remains-high-relative-to-white-workers-in-16-states-and-the-district-of-columbia-the-african-american-unemployment-rate-is-at-least-twice-the-rate-of-white/

11   "MLK Jr.'s Daughter Gets Honest with Hispanic and White Pastors on Divided Church," The Stream, Nov. 11, 2017, https://stream.org/mlk-daughter-divided-church/

12   "Ten Commandments of Nonviolence," Alabama Christian Movement for Human Rights, 1963, http://teachingamericanhistory.org/library/document/commitment-card/

13   "On Views of Race and Inequality, Blacks and Whites Are Worlds Apart," Pew Research Center, Jun. 27, 2016, http://

www.pewsocialtrends.org/2016/06/27/on-views-of-race-and-inequality-blacks-and-whites-are-worlds-apart/

14 "More than 2,000 Attend Service to Discuss Practical Solutions to Racial Divisions," The Reconciled Church, Mar. 20, 2017, https://tinyurl.com/TheReconciledChurch

15 King, Jr., Martin Luther. "Advice for Living," Ebony Magazine, Nov. 1957, https://kinginstitute.stanford.edu/king-papers/documents/advice-living-1

16 "Cape Henry Memorial Cross," National Park Service, Mar. 16, 2016, https://www.nps.gov/came/cape-henry-memorial-cross.htm

17 "The Great Awakening and the American Revolution," Journal of the American Revolution, Aug. 10, 2016, https://allthingsliberty.com/2016/08/great-awakening-american-revolution/

18 "Miracles in America's Past—and Future," Claremont Review of Books, Jan. 23, 2017, http://www.claremont.org/crb/basicpage/miracles-in-americas-pastand-future/

19 "7 Ways Circuit Rider Francis Asbury Showed Us How to Contend Against Injustice," The Christian Post, Apr. 7, 2015, https://www.christianpost.com/news/7-ways-circuit-rider-francis-asbury-showed-us-how-to-contend-against-injustice-137054/

20 "Evangelicals Least Likely to Pay Close Attention to 2016 Campaign," The Barna Group, Mar. 24, 2016, https://www.

barna.com/research/evangelicals-least-likely-to-pay-close-attention-to-2016-campaign/

21 Hayes, Mike, "One Nation Under God," Covenant Church, delivered Oct. 9 and 16, 2016, https://tinyurl.com/One-NationUnderGodMikeHayes

22 "Democratic and Republican Party Platforms," Billy Graham Evangelistic Association, Aug. 23, 2016, https://billygraham.org/story/2016-party-platforms/

23 See Zechariah 2:8

24 "The Statistical Yearbook of Jerusalem, 2018 edition," The Jerusalem Institute for Israel Studies, May 11, 2018, https://tinyurl.com/JerusalemYearbook2018

25 "Pastor Mike Hayes Explains Why We Support Israel," Wall-Builders Live, Aug. 7, 2017, https://wallbuilderslive.com/support-isreal/

26 "The True Face of Christendom," The Jerusalem Post, Feb. 7, 2017, https://www.jpost.com/Blogs/Israel-Uncensored/The-True-Face-of-Christendom-480779

27 Shirer, William, The Rise and Fall of the Third Reich, Simon & Schuster, 1990.

28 Richardson, Joel, "A Simplified Overview of the Covenants," Feb. 23, 2016, https://joelstrumpet.com/a-simplified-overview-of-the-covenants/

29 "Pastor Shares of Devastation in Houston and California — And How People Can Help," The Stream, Oct. 13, 2017,

https://stream.org/pastor-shares-devastation-houston-california-people-can-help/

30   Hayes, Mike, Influence: Becoming the Leader That Changes the World, Mike Hayes Ministries, 2017.

31   "Mike Pence Says His Children Gave Lives to Christ at Billy Graham Crusade," The Christian Post, Feb. 28, 2018,   https://www.christianpost.com/news/mike-pence-says-his-children-gave-lives-to-christ-at-billy-graham-crusade-219747/

32   "The Declaration of Independence," Second Continental Congress, adopted July 4, 1776

33   "The Passing of the WWII Generation," The National World War II Museum, accessed May 21, 2018, https://www.nationalww2museum.org/war/wwii-veteran-statistics

34   "Charlottesville Faith Leaders Unite for Public Prayer to Heal Community Wounds," The Stream, Dec. 4, 2017, https://stream.org/charlottesville-faith-leaders-unite-public-prayer-heal-community-wounds/

CENTER FOR NATIONAL RENEWAL

WASHINGTON, D.C.

WORKING FOR RENEWAL IN OUR NATION BY
UNITING IDEAS AND INFLUENCERS TO
EFFECT CHANGE AND **PROMOTE RECONCILIATION**

→ Join the National Renewal Prayer Network to receive weekly updates

→ Come to Washington, D.C. for a Renewal Tour of key historic sites and revival history

→ Partner With Us to see the vision for renewal spread across the nation

To Receive Weekly E-mail Updates, Text RENEWAL to 41411

Visit CFNR.org to Learn More

about the author

Dr. Mike Hayes is a reconciler. His life and ministry are characterized by connecting people in life-giving relationship with God and each other. He is a uniter—catalyzing racial reconciliation and healing for more than 40 years.

As the Founding Pastor of Covenant Church in Carrollton, Texas, he pioneered a ministry that exemplifies covenant relationships. Flourishing in diversity, with more than 100 nations represented, Covenant Church has become a leading voice for unity and a model for transcultural, multigenerational and multiethnic ministry.

He is the author of several books, including *Influence: Becoming the Leader that Changes the World* and the bestseller *God's Law of First Things*. Dr. Mike Hayes currently serves as President of Churches in Covenant, a global network of churches and ministries united to bless the nations.

In January of 2017, he launched a new initiative focused on bringing hope and restoration to our nation. The Center for National Renewal in Washington D.C. is a Christian, interdenominational, non-partisan organization that seeks to unite ideas and influencers to effect change and promote reconciliation. As a hub of intercession, reconciliation, education and influence, the Center for National Renewal serves to collaborate with local and national leaders to heal the deep divides in our land.

Dr. Mike Hayes and his wife, Kathy, have embarked on a new journey. Together, they are called to leverage decades of ministry and a wealth of influence—to see an unprecedented time of refreshing and renewal sweep across our nation and the world.

other books by
Dr. Mike Hayes

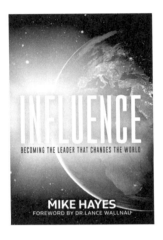

Influence: Becoming the Leader that Changes the World

You are called to lead. From spouses and parents, to business owners and politicians, our world is in need of leaders. The enemy of your soul takes leadership seriously. He knows that you have the potential to do him a vast amount of damage.

Three things—your calling, anointing and leadership gifting—should be subjects of supreme interest in your life. It starts with your calling, what you were born and anointed to do. In 13 power-packed chapters, Dr. Hayes illuminates what it takes for men and women to influence the world.

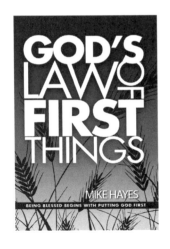

God's Law of First Things

Gods Law of First Things reveals how and why God opens windows of blessings in your life. When you put God first in everything you do and you begin to follow His plan for your life, the doors of opportunity open more readily.

This is a book about learning the joy of giving—and finding how it makes your path ahead clearer. God's Law of First Things is about much more than finances. It is an issue of the heart. Dive into the outpouring of blessings available when God is first.

Order now at MikeHayes.org